# KOREA-U.S.A. CENTENNIAL

## 1882-1982

# KOREA-U.S.A. CENTENNIAL

**Published by:**
Yonhap News Agency
President-Publisher: Kim Seong Jin
PO Box Kwanghwamoon 1039
Seoul, Korea

**Design and Photo-editing:**
Pacific Media, Ltd.
President: Richard K. Sink
CPO Box 7630
Seoul, Korea

**Printing:**
Samhwa Printing Co., Ltd.
CPO Box 1307
Seoul, Korea

Oversize
DS
910. 2
.U6
K6

# KOREA-U.S.A. CENTENNIAL

## 1882-1982

**YONHAP NEWS AGENCY**

SEOUL, KOREA

# PROCLAMATION

## BY THE PRESIDENT
## OF THE REPUBLIC OF KOREA

May 22, 1982 is a very significant date since it marks the 100th anniversary of the building of a bridge of friendship between Korea and the United States. In greeting this felicitous day, I proudly look back on the record of friendship that has deepened and been extended over a century.

In signing a treaty of amity and commerce a century ago, both Korea and America expressed a firm determination to establish ties of eternal friendship and goodwill. This resolution has been translated into rewarding results.

Our two nations, united in a community of destiny as passengers on the same boat bound for a common destination, have helped and cared for each other, working together in peace and peril. In the Korean and Vietnamese Wars in particular, youths from both countries shed their blood, fighting side by side against common enemies. Our two nations have thus built not merely friendship but the strong ties of a blood alliance.

Although our two countries are separated by an ocean, we are very close in political, economic, cultural and security terms. Even though we speak different languages, we have succeeded in minimizing communication difficulties. Although we may have different skin colors, our spirits are akin.

The Korean-American partnership, developed over the past 100 years, stands out as a monument to the common goal of prosperity for all mankind. In that sense, our two peoples can take great satisfaction and deep pride in the centennial.

I believe, however, that today should not merely be an occasion to congratulate ourselves on the accomplishments of the past century; we must also take this occasion to renew our resolve to make the forthcoming century even more rewarding and fruitful.

We share faith in freedom, peace and democracy. To keep this enterprise encourages initiative and innovation. And we both believe that hard work and diligence will lead to a better life and a better world for our children. As we enter this second century of our relationship, we can look with satisfaction on our past accomplishments and with anticipation to the future. We will stand by our friends in Korea. In so doing, we reaffirm our dedication to the principles of freedom and democracy as the basis of our continued strength and friendship. It is fitting,

For the Yonhap News Agency With best wishes, Ronald Reagan

then, that we now reflect upon our relations with this great nation and its people.

NOW, THEREFORE, I, RONALD REAGAN, President of the United States of America, do hereby proclaim the week of May 16 through May 22 as a week of national observance of the centennial of the establishment of diplomatic relations between the United States and Korea and of the ties of friendship that bind our two peoples.

IN WITNESS WHEREOF, I have hereunto set my hand this fifteenth day of May in the year of our Lord nineteen hundred and eighty-two, and of the Independence of the United States of America the two hundred and sixth.

Ronald Reagan

Ronald Reagan
President

# R E S O L U T I O N

n the occasion marking the centennial of diplomatic relations between Korea and the United States of America, the National Assembly of the Republic of Korea,

**Reaffirming** the bonds of friendship based on a common respect for freedom, justice and peace that have long existed between the two peoples of the Republic of Korea and the United States of America;

**Sincerely appreciating** the historical contributions made by the people and the government of the United States of America toward the restoration of the national sovereignty of the Korean people at the end of World War II and later toward the establishment of the government of the Republic of Korea on August 15, 1948;

**Gratefully remembering** the tens of thousands of American officers and men who gave their lives in the defense of freedom and independence of the Republic of Korea, and indeed for world peace;

**Bearing in mind** that the political and military decisions taken by the people and the government of the United States of America to resist the continuing armed threats from North Korea and to bring about peace and stability on the Korean peninsula have been widely acclaimed by all peace-loving people of Korea and of the world:

**Expresses** our profound appreciation for the positive support and cooperation extended by the people and the government of the United States of America in the restoration of the sovereign independence of the Korean people and the subsequent establishment of the government of the Republic of Korea;

**Pays** the highest tribute to the members of the armed forces of the United States of America, who gave their lives in the defense of freedom and peace by resolutely resisting the Communist aggressors during the 1950-53 Korean War, and extends to

their bereaved families our sincere condolences and prayers;

**Desires** the continuous support and cooperation of the people and the government of the United States of America in our efforts to bring about peace, stability, freedom, progress and the early realization of peaceful unification of the Korean peninsula;

**Pledges** to work for further enhancement of friendly and cooperative relations between the peoples and governments of the Republic of Korea and the United States of America in political, economic, cultural, security and all other fields on the basis of reciprocity and equal partnership;

**Decides** on the occasion marking the centennial of diplomatic relations between Korea and the United States of America to present the Plaque of Friendship to the Congress of the United States of America in the name of the Korean people, extolling the bonds of friendship that unite the peoples of our two countries.

# R E S O L U T I O N

xpressing the sense of the U.S. Congress on the occasion of the centennial of the establishment of diplomatic relations between the United States and Korea:

**WHEREAS** May 22, 1982, marks the 100th anniversary of the signing of a treaty of peace, amity, commerce and navigation between the United States of America and Korea;

**WHEREAS** this treaty provided for the formal opening of diplomatic relations between two countries;

**WHEREAS** the American and Korean people have during the past century strengthened the cultural, commercial and security bonds that unite them;

**WHEREAS** Americans sacrificed their lives in assisting the Korean people to defend their freedom against aggression and Koreans fought side-by-side with Americans in Vietnam; and

**WHEREAS** dedication to the principles of freedom and democracy is the basis of the continued strength and friendship of the United States and Korea;

**NOW** therefore, be it resolved by the Senate (House of Representatives concurring): that the Congress hereby—

(1) considers the 100th anniversary of the establishment of diplomatic relations between the U.S. and Korea as an occasion of special historic significance; and

(2) communicates to the National Assembly of the Republic of Korea and to the people of Korea the wishes of the United States Congress and the American people for a peaceful and prosperous future.

한미수교100년1882-1982 · KOREA-USA CENTENNIAL

# C O N T E N T S

# INTRODUCTION

t began with "mutual entanglement in late 19th century imperialism," writes one Asian chronicler, and was "characterized by ignorance and mistrust." Nevertheless, the events of that era, adds another historian, established the "beginning of an association between two peoples, who, although separated by half a globe's distance and by deep cultural and historical differences, were instinctively drawn together. The spark then lighted has never gone out."

The unique ties that bind Korea and America go back a century in time—to 1882 and a treaty formalizing the improbable alliance that, according to a senior American political analyst, "opened the 'Hermit Kingdom' to a variety of interactions with the United States."

In this centennial year it is indeed significant and a measure of the depth of the affinity between Korea and America, that these bonds have endured and been made even stronger by the crises that have threatened them; that they survived the turbulent closing years of the 19th century and America's literal "sell-out" of Korea; that they persisted through the "non-period," as one scholar describes it, of Japanese suppression, during which time the Korean people's desperate cries for liberation went virtually unheeded for 35 years; and that they persevered through the post-World War II years when Korean independence was squelched by events of staggering geopolitical significance that would leave the beleaguered nation devastated by a fratricidal war and tragically divided.

It was during this last disastrous period that the relationship between the two countries was probably put to its most severe test.

It was this time of "unimaginable and unparalleled sacrifices," according to a Southern California professor of history, "that brought Koreans and Americans together more closely than ever before."

And it was out of this "brief eight-year period between 1945 and

1953," he argues, "that the contemporary Korean-American relationship was born."

This relationship, described by U.S. Defense Secretary Caspar Weinberger in an address commemorating the Korean-American centennial anniversary, was founded by mutual security interests which "began in the dark days of the Korean War and were formalized in the Mutual Defense Treaty of 1954," an agreement that persists to this day and has been labeled "the touchstone or bedrock of the Korean-American relationship."

American emergency relief and economic assistance helped raise Korea from the ashes of war and later provided the impetus for the unprecedented economic growth of the 1960s and 1970s.

"No one could have predicted the way it has worked out," says an American economic authority on Korea. "Nor would one have foreseen the growth in Korea's per capita GNP from $80 to more than $1,700, or that of exports from $50 million to $20.7 billion." And "few would have anticipated the end of U.S. aid or the development of an enormous, mutually beneficial trade and investment relationship with the U.S."

But the past three decades were not always smooth between the new-found allies, notes one long-time Korea resident/observer. "Americans had rather rigid ideas of political propriety, and the postwar history of Korea, presenting as it did intolerable pressures and seemingly insurmountable challenges in every area of government and administration, of economies, of national security, was totally without precedent in the American experience."

But neither "the vastness of the Pacific Ocean that separates the two countries nor their different cultural origins" could shake that relationship or "diminish their mutual determination...and common dedication to peace, prosperity and freedom."

In his analysis of "some realities in U.S.-Korean relations," American Ambassador to Korea Richard L. Walker noted, "The years 1979 and 1980 were turbulent and difficult in Korea." During a period of approximately fourteen months, the country experienced the assassination of President Park and the ensuing political turbulence. It was hit by the record oil price shock. A cold and rainy summer brought on the worst rice crop in decades. Inflation reached a 44.3 percent annual rate. Korea faced a formidable challenge and was tested in terms of whether its achievements of the prior two decades were viable. In 1981 the answer was clearly in the affirmative. While many countries, including some of the Western European powers, were recording negative growth, Korea recovered from the losses of 1980 and recorded better than seven percent growth in the national economy for the year. Inflation was more than cut in half."

"To summarize the Korean-American relationship in its totality," concludes the report of the Symposium on Korean-American Relations "is an attempt to paint in bold strokes the advancements of two societies and cultures. It is hoped that a common awareness of the origins and development of these relations will strengthen our mutual ties so that the relationship may endure the trials and turmoil that might challenge it in the future."

It is fitting that in this centennial year Korean-American ties have never been stronger. And, as William M. Carpenter, senior political-military analyst at the Strategic Studies Center (SRI) wrote in summary of the joint communique issued at the conclusion of the meeting between Presidents Chun and Reagan at the White House February 2, 1981, "It is thus highly significant and extremely important both to Korea and the United States that President Chun Doo Hwan came to Washington" as the first foreign head of state to be invited by the new Reagan administration.

"Further, not content to rest on the strength of the existing bonds of friendship, the two presidents wisely noted that 'there remains a need for further promotion of mutual understanding and exchanges between the two peoples through both private and public channels.'

Thus it is not only the two national leaders and their respective officials who have the opportunity and the necessity to strengthen Korean-American friendship; every one of us can make his or her own contribution to the ties that bind together two nations and two peoples who cherish the benefits of freedom."

*Republic of Korea President Chun Doo Hwan and U.S. President Ronald Reagan reaffirmed the bonds of Korean-American friendship and cooperation during President Chun's visit to the White House Feb. 2, 1981.*

King Kojong
26th Monarch of Yi Dynasty
1864-1907

Chester A. Arthur
21st President of the U.S
1881-1885

Min Yong Ik
First Korean envoy to the U.S
1883-1884

Lucius Foote
First U.S. minister to Korea
1883-1885

# ONE HUNDRED YEARS

## FOUNDATIONS

 one hundred years' survey of Korean-American relations is really in effect a history of modern Korea, according to University of Southern California Professor Michael Robinson who explains the background of the relationship. "It was only in the changed realities of late 19th century East Asian politics that the Hermit Kingdom had to open her doors, had to begin a system of treaties, a system of relations with the outside world.

"It is unique that Koreans decided that the United States would be their first foreign partner in a new system of international relations of equal nation-states that was not tied to the Sino-centric world view Koreans had maintained for centuries.

"Looking back one hundred years, to the summer of 1882 and the first promulgation of the treaty between the U.S. and Korea, there was a considerable amount of ignorance on both parts and the importance of Korea to the U.S. was rather minimal in the beginning.

"The U.S. had been interested in East Asia, in opening commercial doors to the society of East Asia. Korea had for years been neglected, partly because it was small, partly because Koreans themselves had a self-conscious policy of seclusion up into the 1870s.

"In 1882 the Koreans were interested in a treaty with the United States only really at the behest of their great neighbor China. The importance of the U.S. to Korea in this early period then was only to bring in another foreign barbarian to help balance off the other barbarians that had been clamoring for recognition. And the seclusion policy, it was clear in the early 1880s, was no longer viable in a vastly changed East Asian political situation.

"Throughout the one hundred years of Korean-American rela-

*Facing page: The destinies of Korea and America became entwined when these men began diplomatic interaction a century ago.*

tions, outside influences have been decisive in pushing each country closer together. In the beginning, Korea and the U.S. were dealing in an era of high imperialism, of predacious Western powers, all vying for spheres of influence in the Far East and, indeed, a militaristic and much more powerful Japan rising in the late nineteenth century.

"It was really Japan that played a decisive role in moving Koreans out of their traditional posture of isolation in East Asia. The rise of Meiji Japan forever changed the power balance in China and in East Asia, and it was really the Chinese-Japanese rivalry that brought Korea into contact with the outside world.

"The Koreans continued through 1876 to refer their primary relationships and responsibilities to China and the Western powers were rather confused as to what to do. In the 1860s and 1870s, they would arrive on the shores of Korea and send messages to the royal house, never to be received by more than a coastal county magistrate. They would then be informed that Korea really could not have autonomous or bilateral relationships with the Western barbarians because the Koreans were subservient to China and that the Americans should go talk to the Chinese. The Westerners would go talk to the Chinese and the Chinese would say no, that Korea was not their property. Korea was autonomous and independent and so back and forth went the Western traders and commercial envoys, trying to figure out just what Korea's status was."

## STORMY BEGINNINGS

It was on one such voyage in 1866 that the American merchant ship, the General Sherman, sailed up the Taedong River toward Pyongyang, now the capital of North Korea, obstensibly to establish trade. But the Korean officials who encountered the General Sherman

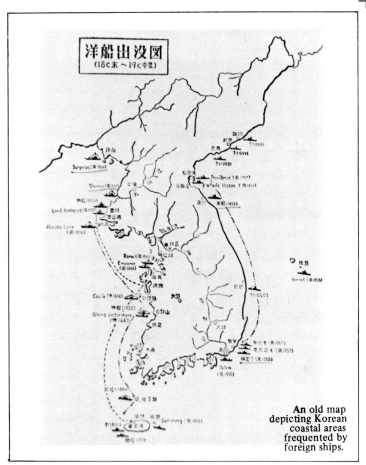

An old map depicting Korean coastal areas frequented by foreign ships.

were suspicious that the real objective of the Americans was to rob the ancient tombs of their kings. Moreover, following a bloody anti-Christian movement in which nine French Catholic priests and several thousand Korean converts had been persecuted, there reportedly was a rumor among the Koreans that the French would launch a retaliatory invasion.

Considering those circumstances, the Korean officials ordered the crew to leave immediately.

The General Sherman, however, continued toward Pyongyang, taking in custody a Korean commander who had tried to prevent the ship from sailing on.

About nine days later, the ship ran aground and the uneasy crew provoked the local inhabitants, killing seven and injuring five others. Enraged over the incident, the Koreans burned the ship and massacred its 24 crewmen.

A joint American-French force to Korea was subsequently contemplated but failed to materialize. And after an attempt to settle the incident and establish proper diplomatic and commercial relations through Japanese assistance failed, U.S. Secretary of State William Seward ultimately dispatched the U.S.S. Colorado and four other ships from the American Asiatic fleet, under the joint command of

Rear Admiral John Rodgers and Frederick Low, the American minister to China. The expedition anchored off Inchon and attempted to make contact, to no avail. A survey party then approached Kanghwa Island and was fired on by Korean naval forces. The ensuing clashes resulted in what is known in Korea as the *Shin-mi Yang-yo,* or the "1871 American Incursion," in which 350 Koreans were killed.

Americans withdrew the following day, their "gunboat diplomacy" successful only in reaffirming the Korean government's anti-Western stance.

## THE AMERICAN INCURSION

*Facing page (from top): The U.S.S. Flagship Colorado anchored on the Salee River; U.S. Marines from the Colorado after capturing Mt. McKee (Chojijin Fortress) on Kanghwa Island; A council of war aboard the Colorado. Left: Korean soldiers delivering dispatches, aboard the Colorado; below, Korean casualties of the U.S. attack on Kanghwa.*

In 1876 Korea signed its first Western-style agreement, the Kangwha Treaty with Japan.

The 12-article treaty was presented unilaterally by the Japanese to control existing diplomatic relations on the Korean peninsula. As part of the treaty, a trade accord and customs agreement were signed, providing Japan an opening for increased control in Korea.

Professor Michael Robinson analyzed Korea's situation: "It was only after Japan had risen as an emerging power in East Asia that the Chinese decided that they had to negate Japanese interests in Korea. And it was really Lee Heung Jang, a great statesman of the mid and late nineteenth century in China, who decided that he had to take a strong role in putting Korea into the new system as it had been created in East Asia.

"The Chinese wanted to allow the Koreans to maneuver and figured the diplomatic technique of balancing off the Western barbarians' interests should be reaffirmed at this period. This method of taking care of a powerful barbarian with many small barbarians was appealing to the Koreans who were able to understand the idea and also had some interests in diluting Japanese designs in some rather aggressive overtures toward them after 1876.

"It was really serendipitous that Commodore Shufeldt was on the scene in the early 1880s. He had been sent on the flagship "Ticonderoga" to the Far East to expand U.S. commercial interests and to possibly write treaties of friendship with nations whom the U.S. had no recognition of. Shufeldt's arrival in China was taken by Lee Heung Jang as a great opportunity and Lee put the Koreans and Americans together.

"The result of all this was two years of secret diplomacy and correspondence between Peking, Washington and Seoul until finally the 1882 treaty was ratified in fourteen articles."

*Commodore Robert W. Shufeldt established the first fruitful U.S. diplomatic contacts with Korea through the Chinese in 1880 and was able to finalize the Treaty of Peace, Amity, Commerce and Navigation in 1882.*

## THE FIRST KOREA-USA TREATY

"The Koreans were delighted with this treaty because it did provide some counterbalance to Japanese interests," according to Professor Michael Robinson. It also held the line, a very important line to them, because it had no mention for protection of missionaries or right of proselytism of Christianity—something still in the nineteenth century the Korean government, the Yi Dynasty, was very worried about—the spread of heterodox Christianity, heterodox thought in Korea.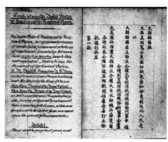

"Article One was a standard article for treaties of that period, which called for peace and friendship between the two nations and also the "good offices clause," that if either nation were threatened, the other nation with its good offices would go to meet the threat.

"They prohibited opium traffic. The king's right was declared to be rice exports (one of the major Korean concerns that foodstuffs would be sucked out of Korea by trade). They also agreed to exchange students and English and Chinese were declared the major languages of communication between both nations.

"Two clauses were slipped through which the Koreans were not particularly worried about nor really even understood the implications of. One was the right of "extraterritoriality" in which foreign envoys, foreign commercial traders, would not be under Korean law, until such time as Korean law was brought into accordance with American legal practice. Another clause that the Koreans did not think about too much, because it was not in their scheme of thinking, was a "most favored nation clause," which granted the Americans rights to the treaty of any other nation put together with Korea, that is, there could be no other treaty granting other countries benefits exceeding those between the U.S. and Korea."

## THE FIRST 30 YEARS

Koreans viewed the Shufeldt Treaty "as a wedge to counter age-old attempts at domination of the kingdom," writes University of Missouri political science professor, Cho Soon Sung.

"When Lucius H. Foote, first envoy extraordinary and minister plenipotentiary of the U.S. arrived at Seoul in May 1883, the king of Korea literally 'danced with joy'."

Foreign intrigues were often dramatic. The concession-hungry maladies of European powers hoping to impose their wills and interests on the beleaguered kingdom resulted in unending, seemingly unlimited, claims, according to Cho.

Among China, Russia, Britain, France, Germany and Japan, a political tug-of-war was going on in Asia in the late 1800s and early 1900s, with Korea the hotly sought-after spoils.

Korea's first Western ally, the United States of America, gave notice to Japan and China not to "infringe upon the kingdom's independence and sovereignty." And an American military training mission arrived at King Kojong's request and trained an elite palace guard while modernizing the regular military forces.

During the turbulent periods before the Russo-Japanese War that ultimately settled power plays and sealed the Yi Dynasty's fate, Americans in Korea were the most ardent supporters of Korean independence, notes the Missouri University professor.

That support ended when Japan won the 1904 war with Russia.

*Facing page: A copy of the original 1882 Treaty of Peace, Amity, Commerce and Navigation. Above: Yi Dynasty militia undergo an inspection in Seoul. They were trained by a four-man American Military Advisory Mission commissioned by King Kojong in the late 1880s*

*Top left: U.S. President Theodore Roosevelt, who agreed to recognize Japanese control of Korea's foreign affairs leading to the conclusion of the Taft-Katsura Agreement; Top right: King Kojong's personal letter to Roosevelt in June 1906 appealing for Korean sovereignty; Above: Japanese Prime Minister Taro Katsura, and (right) U.S. Secretary of War William H. Taft.*

## THE TAFT-KATSURA AGREEMENT

If it was unfortunate that the Old Kingdom was unprepared for the distressing international events culminating with the Russo-Japanese War, situational changes with a new Washington administration would prove even more tragic.

"The attitude of the American government toward Korea changed abruptly under Theodore Roosevelt's administration," says Cho Soon Sung, University of Missouri political science professor. America's rough rider unreservedly favored Japanese control over Korea and ignored a personal request by King Kojong to save his country.

American envoy Dr. Horace Allen hurried to Washington to enlist U.S. assistance after Japan had won the war with Russia, but Korean pleas for help were shattered when Allen found no sympathy in Roosevelt's pro-Japanese cabinet.

Roosevelt ardently supported Japan's domination of Korea as a means to check the Russian drive for Manchuria and Korea's icefree ports, chronicles Cho. The U.S. President told his state department, "We cannot possibly interfere (on behalf of the Koreans) against Japan."

Thus, at a time when Korea desperately needed American help once promised, a secret agreement between then Japanese Prime Minister Katsura and U.S. Secretary of War Taft officially sanctioned Japan's jurisdiction over Korea in return for Japanese disinvolvement in the Philippines.

America's legation pulled out of Seoul as Japan formalized its protectorate status of Korea in 1905, dealing directly with Japan on Korean-related matters. Full annexation and loss of Korean sovereignty five years later saw the U.S. quietly acquiesce.

The death knell of American influence and interest for the next three and one-half decades was sounding.

## JAPANESE OCCUPATION

After Japanese annexation in 1910, Korea was all but forgotten by America until 1919. The United States' involvement in World War I and Wilson's subsequent pronouncement of the self-determination of nations during the peace settlements, gave new hope for independence to the Korean people. The Korean leaders received President Wilson's fourteen points with great enthusiasm and felt certain that a courageous mass uprising of Koreans would win sympathy from America and recognition by the League of Nations.

Taking advantage of the imperial funeral of the Emperor Kojong, who was rumored to have been poisoned by the Japanese, the Korean leaders proclaimed Korean Independence on March 1, 1919 in a public park in Seoul and massive demonstrations began. They were well planned: it was to be a passive revolt.

Millions of Koreans participated throughout the country and the insurrections continued for more than a year before they were ruthlessly suppressed by the Japanese army and police. Troops charged upon crowds, firing guns, swinging swords and pursuing helpless victims. Groups huddled in churches were burned to death.

But the demonstrations had already achieved a notable triumph. The Korean leaders drew up plans for a provisional republic and adopted a provisional constitution. Dr. Syngman Rhee, disciple and personal friend of President Wilson was chosen as president. Thus was born the longest-lived government-in exile in modern history.

Although ruthless measures employed by the Japanese to stamp out the Korean independence movement aroused humanitarian protests from the missionaries and other foreigners residing in Korea, there was no official intervention from any foreign government at the peace conference in Paris. The direct appeal to President Wilson by the Korean leaders brought not a single official response.

Thus, the Korean independence movement was suppressed by the

Japanese without interference from the United States or any participants of the Paris Peace Conference. Korea had become virtually a forgotten nation.

In fact, the United States government failed to concern itself seriously with the Korean question until the end of 1943.

## POST WW II EVOLVEMENTS

The Japanese surprise attack on Pearl Harbor had brought a sudden and significant change in American policy toward Korea. In 1943 the Cairo Declaration by the three wartime leaders, Roosevelt, Churchill and Chiang Kai Shek, provided a ray of hope to the Korean people for the first time in three decades of humiliation. The declaration that "in due course Korea shall become free and independent" was received with great enthusiasm by the Korean people. This declaration not only promised the formal return of diplomatic status to the peninsula, but also expressed U.S. commitment to a free and independent Korea.

When President Roosevelt and his military advisors were planning post-war strategy, Korea was still considered strategically unimportant. Roosevelt's personal opinion was that it would be necessary to educate the Koreans on the model of the Philippines. Thus, at Cairo, he proposed forty years of political tutelage and then, at the Yalta Conference, shortened this period to "from twenty to thirty years."

*Above: So Chae Pil (center) and other delegates to the Pan Pacific Conference at Hawaii in 1925 continued to strengthen independence movement efforts until Korea's liberation in 1945.*

## THREE CONFERENCES

Korea's "enslavement" by the Japanese was criticized at the November, 1943 Cairo Conference at which China, the U.S. and Britain declared that"...Korea shall become free and independent." U.S. President Roosevelt and the Soviet Union's Marshal Stalin formulated a three-power trusteeship of Korea at the February 1945 Yalta Discussion and in July the Potsdam Declaration by China, America and Great Britain set terms for Japanese surrender and reaffirmed Cairo's decision for a free and independent Korea.

The Soviets concurred when they declared war on Japan in August 1945.

Right: America's Franklin D. Roosevelt and China's Chiang Kai Shek at the Cairo Conference. Below: Stalin, Roosevelt and Churchill at the Yalta Conference.

The 38th Parallel had never been subject to international discussion. It was neither bargained for nor debated, but, in late summer of 1945, planners in Washington anxiously monitoring the Russian push into Korea, noted on a map that both Seoul and the major port city of Pusan were located south of the parallel.

"It was intended to be purely a military demarcation of a temporary nature to facilitate the surrender of the Japanese forces in Korea," recalled Dean Rusk, who was pivotal in planning the division policy.

The U.S. opted to curb Soviet occupation of Korea and announced its intention of repatriating Japanese south of the 38th Parallel, even though Harry Truman and the state department had no concrete policy for an American occupation of Korea.

Americans arriving with General John Hodge, commander of the American Occupation Forces in Korea, found a people brutalized from 35 years of unchecked colonialism, a non-existent economy with non-existent industry and a land with barren hills, with soil and fisheries exhausted by exploitation.

Language and cultural differences, insufficient information and a lack of experience and training in military government caused critical problems. And despite America's good intentions, the Korean people began to view the U.S. occupation with suspicion and discontent. The Koreans anticipated their long-awaited independence; the U.S. insisted upon a trusteeship.

A joint American-Soviet commission was formed to take steps toward unifying the divided nation, but, after 24 fruitless sessions it was adjourned indefinitely in May 1946. The failure prompted the U.S. to request the United Nations to establish a unified Korean government with the multi-national organization to assume most of the responsibility.

The UN General Assembly adopted a resolution calling for UN commission-supervised elections throughout Korea. The Soviets denied the commission entry to the North and, as a result, the Republic of Korea was established in the South August 15, 1948.

*General of the Army Douglas MacArthur inspects U.N. forces on the front lines following the Inchon Landing.*

The Soviet command, in defiance of the UN, established the Democratic People's Republic of Korea in Pyongyang, splitting the nation in two and despite the opposition of the Korean people, two governments were created by power politics.

Because of American non-commitment and failure to perceive the real threat toward the Republic of Korea, the South Korean army was totally unprepared at the outbreak of the Korean War on June 25, 1950. Just two weeks earlier, Secretary of State Dean Acheson had announced the American defense perimeter as "extending south from Japan through the Ryukyu Islands." That excluded Korea and many believe in retrospect that the statement was an invitation for North Korea's Soviet-backed invasion.

*U.S. Lt. Gen. Hodges (left) plans the first U.S.-Soviet Commission Meeting with Soviet Marshal Shtykov (right).*

The heart-breaking Korean War began at the 38th Parallel and ended along roughly the same line with an armistice agreement signed July 27, 1953.

What had started as an arbitrary demarcation line hastily drawn by planners in Washington eight years earlier had solidified into a political barrier, center of world tension, and the permanent division of Korea. Some 36,000 Americans were among the

*Republic of Korea President Syngman Rhee (right) with Gen. MacArthur (center) and Lt. Gen. Hodges at a ceremony turning control over to the new government.*

57,000 lives lost by the United Nations Command and civilian deaths were estimated in the millions.

## MAINTAINING PEACE

Never again would there be a half-hearted policy of military commitment to Korea and, as military vigilance was maintained along the uneasy border, a close friendship developed with the Korean people.

U.S. efforts since then have centered on preventing Armistice Agreement violations and restoration of the war-battered Korean economy. Besides concluding the 1954 Mutual Defense Treaty with the Republic of Korea, the U.S. also provided great infusions of economic aid for reconstruction.

Since the Korean War, at no time has any American administration, Republican or Democrat, ever deviated from a policy of strong commitment.

With the help of American military and economic aid, South Korea emerged from the rubbles of war to a proud, industrialized nation.

# KOREANS IN AMERICA

## EARNING A PLACE IN AMERICAN SOCIETY

 hundred years have yet to pass since the first Koreans ventured forth as immigrants to the United States and within that time Koreans in America have developed one of the most successful new ethnic societies in the United States.

The second largest group of overseas Koreans in the world (only China reports a larger ethnic Korean population), Korean-Americans as individuals and as a group have earned the respect of their new nation—just as their homeland has developed and earned its place as an independent and respected member of the world community.

Los Angeles Mayor Thomas Bradley, leader of the city with the world's largest concentration of Koreans overseas, recalled his 1979 visit to Korea, "I found the Korean people friendly, industrious and concerned about other people in their country and throughout the world. Korean-Americans in Los Angeles have contributed those same qualities to our city."

They are "hard working people who have a great respect for our government and its laws," observed New York City Mayor Edward I. Koch, who added that Korean-Americans have also provided a stabilizing community force. And they have been equally successful individually, explained U.S. Ambassador to Korea Richard L. Walker, as "leading academics, cultural figures, artists and architects, businessmen and industrialists and contributors to civic improvement. The successful participation in the American dream by our fellow Korean-Americans is at once an indication of their own talents and an indication of our respect for them."

*The life of the 104-year-old hero of the documentary film, "To the Last Day," the late Yang Choo Eun (facing page), symbolizes the spirit and perseverence of Korean immigrants to America during the past century.*

# FIRST ENCOUNTERS

The Koreans' first encounters in the United States nearly a century ago were relatively brief, but enlightening. Only a handful of diplomats, scholars, businessmen and political refugees discovered America during the late 1800s but their impressions provided the impetus for a fragmented but eventful migration that would affect the destinies of two nations.

Much of the history of Korean immigrants to the United States, on which the following historical accounts are based, has been consolidated by Choy Bong Youn, a professor at Seoul National University, in his book "Koreans in America."

The early encounters and migrations began when the first Koreans landed in the United States Sept. 2, 1883 on an official goodwill mission led by Min Yong Ik.

Yu Kil Jun, a member of that first mission, remained behind to become the first Korean student in America. He studied Western history and the American political system before returning to Korea via Europe. His written account, "Soyu Kyon Mun," or "What I Saw and Heard During My Visit to the West," inspired many Korean intellectuals to travel abroad to learn more about Western culture.

Diplomats and scholars were not the only Koreans drawn to the United States during those early years. Political refugees also found a haven in the new land. So Chae Pil, Park Young Hyo and So Kwang

*Facing page: (top) the first goodwill mission from Korea to the U.S. led by Min Yong Ik; (bottom) the first Korean woman to visit America. Above: Yu Kil Jun, Korea's first student in America.*

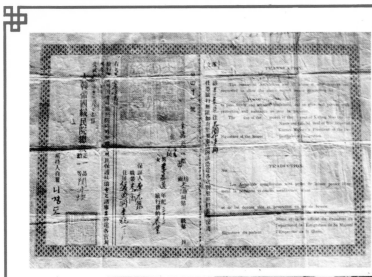

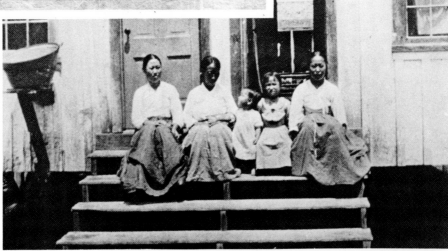

Pum reached the U.S. via Japan following an unsuccessful Korean political coup.

Only the youngest, So Chae Pil, also known as Philip Jaisohn, remained to become Korea's first American-educated medical doctor.

So summarized the feelings and experience of most Koreans in the U.S. during the early years: "We don't speak English; we do not know anybody; we do not have any money. Nobody recognizes us and nobody pays attention to us. We feel like lonely and pitiable abandoned orphans from the ship which carried us across the Pacific."

So returned to his homeland in 1895 to help form Korea's Independence Society, a progressive political party that influenced many young men who would later become noteworthy political leaders.

At the same time the first seeds of democracy were being sown by So and other politically progressive Koreans, the reigning monarch, King Kojong, sent the first resident Korean minister to the United States. Park Chung Yang's arrival in Washington D.C. marked the establishment of an independent Korean legation in 1896.

The first Korean businessman in America was Paik Jang Hing, a ginseng merchant who landed at Honolulu in 1898. Five other ginseng merchants arrived the next year launching the first Korean business ventures in the U.S.

*Facing page (top to bottom): Passport issued by the Yi Dynasty to one of the first Korean immigrants to Hawaii; an early immigrant family in Hawaii; a pineapple plantation worker. Above, congregation at Hawaii's first Korean church.*

At the turn of the century the U.S. Bureau of Immigration recorded the arrival of the first official Korean immigrant. Peter Ryu and 17 others were admitted to Hawaii between 1901 and 1902. They were the first arrivals of what became the largest official pre-war Korean migration to America.

More than 7,000 Korean laborers were drawn to Hawaiian plantations between 1903 and 1905 by American missionaries' glowing accounts of the new land of opportunity. The political and economic strife ravaging Korea was an added inducement.

Most laborers landed in Hawaii without families, following a "dream" in which high wages and a pleasant climate would make their temporary stays bearable, if not enjoyable, while accumulating their fortunes for the return to Korea.

But long, hot work days were only interrupted by equally long nights of drinking, gambling and loneliness. The morale of the Korean laborers became a major problem, one which brought about the "picture bride" program. Picture brides, hundreds of young women who voluntarily traveled to America to wed men they knew only from photographs, comprised the secondary group of immigrants to America in the 1900s.

The early Americans became the nucleus of a developing community, one that except for a few hundred student refugees, grew little numerically until the end of World War II, but blossomed in spirit to provide the base for one of America's most respected ethnic minorities.

*Facing page (top left): The first public school for Korean immigrants in Hawaii; (top right) Honolulu's first Korean church; (middle) immigrants at a 1914 social gathering on the "Korean Compound" in Hawaii; (bottom) the graduation party of Hawaii's first Korean high school.*

*Paek Man Kuk (inset), the second Korean immigrant in Hawaii to marry a picture bride, Paek Myong Sun (above).*

## PICTURE BRIDES

Stories are still told in Hawaii of the Korean "picture brides" who fainted when they arrived in America to discover their future husbands were much uglier or older than the photos which had lured the young women across the Pacific.

Of the 7,000 laborers who traveled to the United States between 1903 and 1905, about 80 percent were bachelors. Their days were occupied with strenuous plantation work, but their nights were filled with "drinking, gambling and sometimes fighting among themselves," according to Choy Bong Youn's book "Koreans in America."

Not surprisingly, marriage became a prime issue. There were no single Korean women in Hawaii and interracial marriage was taboo. With the approval of the U.S. Immigration Service and plantation owners, a program used earlier to get wives for Chinese and Japanese laborers was instituted. "Picture brides" were urged to select prospective mates from photos workers sent families in Korea.

Since many men sent photos taken earlier, or in more favorable circumstances, the blushing brides often reddened in shock at their first face-to-face encounters with men who bore little resemblance to their introductory photographs.

But most brides adjusted to their new mates and country. Many also urged their husbands to leave the plantations and open businesses or buy farms. Their stabilizing force helped the Korean-American community grow economically and socially.

*An ID card issued by the Korean Commission in the United States to Mrs. Kim Shin Suk, now 78, an original "picture bride" married at 18 without knowing her future mate.*

## INDEPENDENCE MOVEMENT

Early Korean immigrants settling in the new land faced many difficulties, not the least of which was survival. But even as they adapted to American life and culture, their hearts and minds were on their homeland.

Korea was in the midst of a multi-national power struggle when immigration to the U.S. began. China, Russia and Japan were all trying to gain control of the Hermit Kingdom.

As early as 1906, Koreans living in Hawaii appealed to President Theodore Roosevelt to help preserve Korea's autonomy against Japanese subordination and insure "that other powers shall not oppress or maltreat our people."

America's community banded together to garner more political support for occupied Korea with organizations such as the Korea National Association in America and the Korean Information Bureau.

The Korean Information Bureau, the official representative of the Korean provisional government in Shanghai, also conducted the "Liberty Congress" in Philadelphia in 1919 to emphasize Korea's cry for independence. And military training camps were established to train young Korean-Americans for active resistance against the Japanese.

---

*Facing page (clockwise from top left): Syngman Rhee at the first Korean Congress in Philadelphia; the Korean delegation to the first congress marching through Philadelphia's Independence Square; Korean Congress delegates in front of the Little Theater; The Korean Revolution Army in the U.S. with founder Park Yong Man (seated center). Above: Ahn Chang Ho (seated center) and leaders of the Korean National Association.*

## INDEPENDENCE LEADERS

Most if not all Koreans living in America during the Japanese occupation of Korea from 1910 were gravely concerned about the fate of their homeland. The U.S. had become a haven for a number of nationalist exiles, who along with many Korean-Americans were actively involved in their countrymen's struggle for independence. Among them perhaps the most prominent were So Chae Pil (Philip Jaisohn), Ahn Chang Ho, Syngman Rhee and Park Yong Man, whose consolidated efforts added real impetus and direction to the movement.

Each, with the exception of So, formed his own political group.

So Chae Pil, a senior statesman, helped form the Independence Society, an organization of young Korean reformists, and established the "Independent" newspaper in Korea. He later formed the Korea Information Bureau in the U.S.

Ahn Chang Ho, one of Korea's most gifted intellectuals, led many Korean independence efforts before being imprisoned in Korea for anti-Japanese activities.

Dr. Syngman Rhee, a Princeton graduate and major spokesman for the movement, helped establish Korea's Independence Society and mustered support for the Korean cause throughout the U.S. In 1948 he became Korea's first president.

Park Yong Man, who believed military action against Japan was the surest way of restoring independence, helped establish military training camps in the U.S. to prepare young Koreans for underground work in their homeland.

*Facing page (clockwise from left): Park Yong Man; Ahn Chang Ho; and So Chae Pil (Philip Jaisohn). Above, Syngman Rhee.*

## WARTIME CONTRIBUTIONS

The dual concerns of most Koreans in America—the Japanese occupation of their homeland and the adaptation to a new land and culture—were unexpectedly melded on the Day of Infamy, Dec. 7, 1941. America was thrown into a war with Korea's worst enemy and Koreans were eager to take part in U.S. action against the Asian war machine.

By coincidence or prophetic forethought, the Korean Commission in the U.S. had won approval for individuals to register as Koreans rather than Japanese subjects just three months before Pearl Harbor. This action probably saved Koreans from the Japanese relocation camps and allowed them to serve in the U.S. armed forces.

While young Koreans were fighting in the Pacific theater, older men and women worked as national guardsmen, fire wardens, Red Cross workers and USO volunteers, or helped sell war bonds. Some 250 Japanese-speaking Koreans served as interpreters for the Office of War Information or as underground agents in the Pacific.

*Facing page (clockwise from top left): Koreans living in Hawaii present $26,265.35 for the war effort to Hawaiian Military Governor Robert C. Richardson; Susan Ahn at 15, eldest daughter of Korean patriot Ahn Chang Ho. She became the first Oriental woman to serve as a U.S. Navy officer during WWII; the California National Guard's Tiger Unit, comprised of Korean-Americans, formed in the wake of the attack on Pearl Harbor; Korean-American Red Cross volunteers. Above, a Korean-American in uniform.*

# MONUMENTS TO THE EARLY IMMIGRANTS

Much of Korean-American history is reflected in historic sites and buildings that still exist today—from the plantations of Hawaii to residential Washington, D.C.— monuments to the efforts of the early immigrants who laid the foundations of the Korean community in the U.S. Here they launched the independence movement, established organizations for ethnic development and centered their first U.S. diplomatic involvements.

*Facing Page (clockwise from top left): Philadelphia's Independence Hall, where Korea's independence declaration was read in 1919; Plays and Players (former Little) Theater, site of the first Korean Congress; the first Korean legation building in Washington, D.C. At right: The First Korean National Association Center in L.A. Below: a Hawaiian sugar cane plantation on Oahu where the first immigrants worked.*

# THE NEW IMMIGRANTS

A new wave of immigrants began entering the United States after World War II. By 1965 the pre-war Korean-American population had tripled, with more than 16,000 Korean immigrants and some 5,000 students (many of whom changed their status to residents) during the 20-year period. The influx heralded the beginning of a new era for the Korean-American community which would grow to more than 700,000 over the next 17 years.

Encouraged by relaxation of immigration laws in 1965 when President Lyndon B. Johnson repealed the National Origin Quota System of 1924, upwards to 30,000 Koreans annually migrate to America. Their numbers represent the largest national group, aside from Filipinos, to immigrate to the U.S. since World War II.

The exodus from Korea which picked up momentum in 1971, was promoted by a number of factors according to Choy Bong Youn in his book, "Koreans in America."

"...The South Korean government encouraged people to immigrate," partially, he observed, because of the country's dense population and the strain it was putting on the land and economy.

He also cited the political uncertainty of the divided peninsula, the fear of war and the more restrictive political structure of the time. The situation in Korea "impelled many discontented intellectuals and professionals to leave South Korea."

These intellectuals and professionals represented an important segment of the new immigrants. Early immigrants, said Choy, planned to return to their homeland. "The new immigrants were here to stay"—to educate their children and make better lives for themselves.

*Successful innovator and entrepreneur, Philip Whang (facing page) exemplifies the new immigrants ability to overcome social and cultural barriers in their pursuit of "the American dream."*

## KOREATOWNS

The new wave of Korean immigrants to "the land of opportunity" has precipitated another socio-economic phenomenon—the emergence, nationwide, of urban Korean communities called "Koreatowns."

Like cultural islands in the midst of metropolitan American cities, their boundaries subtly delineated by a preponderance of "Hangul" (Korean phonetic characters) billboards and signs, these inner cities provide a protective shield against their unfamiliar, often hostile urban surroundings. They offer a friendly face to Koreans new to the U.S. and a cultural refuge for those that stay.

Here, insulated from the social, cultural and communication barriers of mainstream America, the newly-arrived can shop, visit the dentist, read a newspaper and order a meal—all without having to speak or read a word of English.

And here, in the hearts of Los Angeles, New York, Chicago—from Honolulu to Baltimore—America's Koreans have established the roots of one of the most impressive ethnic success stories in U.S. immigration history.

Their Koreatowns are the foundations of "a stabilizing community force" and the basis for their collective self-reliance, which has earned them recognition as "America's model minority."

*Facing page: The world's largest overseas ethnic Korean community, Koreatown in Los Angeles has earned official recognition warranting municipal sign identification. Above (clockwise from top left): Koreatowns in Los Angeles, New York, San Francisco and Chicago.*

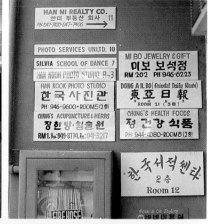

## THE NEW MERCHANTS

For many Korean immigrants, arrival in America means culture shock and a struggle for economic survival.

Many have come from high income or at least solid middle class environments and have often left prestigious or comparatively high-paying jobs to travel to the "land of opportunity." Most arrive with at least meager savings which are often invested in small business ventures to establish a solid foundation.

But many times the unfamiliar culture, often confusing bureaucracy and general misgivings about their new environment hamper their attainment of "instant success." Innately tenacious however, Koreans strive for self-sufficiency and their perseverence often pulls them through difficulties which would defeat others.

The familiar and comfortable surroundings of Koreatowns are often the starting points. Immigrants lean toward the familiarity of enterprises common in their homeland and which often require more manual input than monetary investment: Korean restaurants; small markets or produce stores; Taekwondo schools; electronic stores; and Oriental medical centers are popular among beginning entrepreneurs.

If successful they move with confidence, out of the Koreatowns and into the mainstream of America.

---

*Facing page: From Atlanta to Honolulu, Korean business enterprises are as widespread as they are diverse and, like Mrs. Kim J. Yong's Korean restaurant (above), they underscore the firm belief that the "American dream" is possible for anyone who works hard for it.*

*The wig business was a popular enterprise for many Korean immigrants in the early 1970s and was the road to success for Lee Sung Kyu, owner of Lee's Wig Shop in Athens, Georgia, shown above with his wife in front of their suburban home.*

*Jim Hwang became the first Korean-American GM (General Motors) dealer in the U.S., starting with only $300. In 14 years he built up a million dollar-plus business.*

*Jung Doo Shin, another successful Korean businessman-merchant, owns the Camera World Building (above) and the largest camera shop in Portland, Oregon.*

## 'THE AMERICAN DREAM' By Cho Wha You

Former U.S. Ambassador to the United Nations Andrew Young, a member of the Black ethnic minority once said, "People say America is a melting pot. But I say this country is not a melting pot. It is rather a stew with each ingredient and spice contributing to the taste and flavor of the whole." Koreans in America certainly have been and are contributing to the American "stew" with their own ingredients of hard-work, brains and cultural heritage.

The well-educated and hard-working Korean immigrants are welcome almost universally throughout the U.S. Despite the language barriers and culture shock, most of them quickly adapt to the new environments.

From a Mr. Hwang in San Francisco who became a millionaire in the electronics industry to a Mr. Lee who owns a mom-and-pop grocery store in Houston, the Koreans in America regard their adopted country as a land of opportunity, as did the earlier European immigrants. They believe the American dream is possible for anyone who works diligently. And many Korean families have already made their American dream come true.

Korean-Americans are prominent in almost every sector of American society...in the academic world, fine arts, science and technology, business, banking, literature, journalism, and even in the sports and entertainment worlds.

Still brighter prospects are the second generation of Korean immigrants. Their intelligence and talent are generally recognized not only in high schools in major cities but also in famous colleges all over the United States.

As Korean-American relations enter the second century, the youngsters of Korean heritage will obviously become the seeds for developing better ties and a deeper mutual understanding between both countries.

# SOME KOREAN-AMERICAN REALITIES
## By K. W. Lee

*K.W. Lee, investigative reporter for the Sacramento Union and editor of "Koreatown."*

Only a few years ago Koreans loomed in America's mega-media as sinister aliens bearing gifts and bribes to subvert the Congress of the United States. The KCIA, Tong Sun Park and the moonfaced Reverend Moon were headline makers and the objects of investigative reporting. Hapless Koreans in America, who had nothing to do with the influence-buying scandal, underwent a psychological "concentration camp" period during those frenzied, media-hyped hysteria years.

Almost every one of us bears a...scar.

We remember all too well those bleak years when politicians—and bureaucrats—avoided us like yellow plague. Our children lived with cruel jokes and tauntings from their unthinking peers. Korean businesses in inner cities were targets of vicious harassment during the Koreagate years.

Today the Yo-Yo Syndrome—so painfully familiar to the collective memory of California's Asian-Americans in those dark decades past—has hoisted these erstwhile sinister Koreans on a high pedestal, from a helpless scapegoat to a model minority for other minorities, especially blacks and browns, to follow and emulate.

This nation's super-media—the New York Times, Wall Street Journal, Washington Post and Los Angeles Times, to cite a few—have switched their tune whimsically. Hard-working, aggressive, and successful, and a stabilizing force in inner cities. Out of the blue we've become a super-minority of sorts.

Listen to this almost rhapsodic report in the Wall Street Journal:

*"The Koreans are showing that the way to honorably suc-*
*ceed in America is through the old-fashioned virtues of toil*
*and self-sacrifice. Their ability to overcome cultural and*
*social distance with little or no assistance challenges one*
*assumption entrenched for years in the federal bureaucracy*
*that the minorities need special attention and billions of*
*dollars in loans and set-aside government contracts to place*
*them at a par with most white Americans."*

Koreans are a remarkably hardy people who can suffer a great deal without rancor, but obviously they don't have the monopoly on these ancient virtues. Neither have they—imprisoned in their own language barriers—overcome the cultural and social distance with the mainstream. The bureaucracy has ignored the Koreans who have no clout.

There's a surrealistic "Alice in Korea Town" air about this media-spawned Korean success story born of benign ignorance, indifference and insensitivity to the new immigrants.

As half-truths always are, this success story is only partially true. The untold side of this saga is that the new immigrants from Korea have had to fall on their own wit, guts and resources for their daily and hourly survival in their adopted land. And they are paying dearly for it.

The reality of emerging "Korea Towns" across this continent has been subterranean and existential—melancholy behind their impassive facades.

Unseen and unheard, most of these immigrants have found the "American dream" a fantasy or nightmare. Theirs is a strange voice that is not understood or heard by the host society.

As San Francisco reporter Connie Kang, one of a few Korean-born journalists working in the American media, wrote not long ago in the English-language newspaper, "Koreatown:"

> *"For every Korean success story, there are a dozen stories of shattered lives; for every act of Korean heroism, there is at least one act of cowardice; for every beautiful Korean in America, there is his ugly counterpart; for every Korean home that is happy, there are a half dozen that are not."*

Divorces and separations are soaring in geometric progression, as immigrant families are literally falling apart almost overnight under the stress of hostile urban conditions.

The bitter irony of all of this is that most new Korean immigrants—who are the highest educational and occupational group in America's immigration history—generally experience a downward mobility in this land of opportunity because of language and cultural barriers. This downward mobility exacts heavy tolls in every aspect of Korean immigrant life.

The vaunted Korean success story in small businesses is but a form of unrelenting self-exploitation. Husband-wife teams toil 12 to 16 hours a day, seven days a week, to eke out a living. Vacations are unheard of. They are "Kamikazes." Unable to enter the mainstream market they literally risk their lives to open "Mom and Pop" stores in high-crime inner-city districts. Murders, robberies and rapes haunt their lives.

Despite these crippling problems, the Korean communities remain fragmented and divided and incapable of forging unity to deal with the powers that be to help solve them.

Korea Town is not a "community." It's a huge train depot—in constant flux with new arrivals and departures for outlying suburbs.

The emerging Koreans are a disparate bunch. There's only the semblance of a community. In reality it's a mosaic composed of people with different time-frames of values and lifestyles: a few surviving old immigrants and their Americanized children; continuing waves of new immigrants, including the American-educated, the Korean-educated and the uneducated and their children, both American-born and Korean-born; and Korean wives married to American servicemen.

Social and communication gaps are wide and widening among these disparate groups. Non-communication and non-cooperation mark the behaviors of these emerging Korean-Americans. Unity is a remote subject.

And unsettling is the alienation of the English-speaking children from the Korean-speaking parent generation. Korean enclaves are largely geared to the needs of the Korean-speaking adult males.

But all is not gloom and doom. There's a promising prospect in the persistently strong ethnic attachment of these new immigrants, regardless of the lengths of their stay in this country.

Their born-again Koreanness in the new land may provide possibilities of a bicultural life for their offspring as an alternative to the complete assimilation of Japanese-Americans (their "price for... effective Americanization").

Korean immigrants—with structured culture and values from Korea—would indeed have to bolster them as their survival strategy when the host society's institutions—families, neighborhoods and schools—are becoming unhinged.

The redeeming grace of the new immigrants—self-reliant and self-centered—will provide the crucial cocoon for their offspring to grow and become productive in the mainstream, during these stormy times.

Their glorious stamina and stubbornness will provide that margin of sanity in their melancholy journey in America.

## STUDENTS IN AMERICA

Korean-American students represent one group of immigrants who deserve particular recognition. From the earliest years of immigration Koreans have consistently emerged as top academic achievers. Among the first Korean students, many completed college educations in America and a few, including Syngman Rhee, Kim Kyu Sic and Kang Yung Sung, earned their doctorates. Between 1945 and 1965, more than 5,000 students traveled to the U.S. for undergraduate and graduate studies. Today thousands of Korean-American students attend high schools, universities and graduate schools throughout the United States and many have earned academic recognition for their achievements.

*Korean-American students are enrolled in many of America's most prestigious universities. Above: (top left) a Korean-American cadet at West Point Military Academy; (top right) students at the University of Illinois; and (above) a discussion group of Korean students from Harvard and MIT. Facing page: (top right) a Korean-American coed attends a lecture at Georgetown University Law Center and (bottom) a student at Julliard School of Music.*

Many Korean-American students have earned national recognition for their academic and sports achievements, including Pak Hae Su (left), a coed at Douglas University, New Jersey. Pak has won the

North Atlantic Figure Skating Competition every year since 1976 and ranked third in the 1977 Nationals. Katherine Moon, pictured below with Secretary of Defense Caspar W. Weinberger during a tour of the U.S. capital, won a scholarship under the Senate Youth Program for her outstanding academic performance.

College football star Peter Kim led the University of Alabama in scoring, was fifth nation-wide in scoring and held five school records throughout the 1981 season. Former soccer player and brother of the famous Korean woman Olympic basketball player, Kim Myung Cha, he was born in Seoul and may soon become the first Korean-American professional football player.

## REFLECTIONS ON 5,000 YEARS

Korea's centuries-old culture has been a unifying force and focus for ethnic identity in the Korean-American community since the first immigrants entered the United States.

The first Koreans living in America used their language, customs and heritage as a common base for establishing new relationships because they had lost their traditional family ties, according to Dr. Thomas Hosuck Kang, director for the East Asia Research Institute.

Cultural preservation in the early years focused on the basics of security, comraderie and achievement. But as the community became more complex, efforts stressed ethnic pride.

Today cultural activities permeate all facets of community life from Korean-American media to the perpetuation of centuries-old traditions.

Korean-American published newspapers provide a community voice. Neighborhood schools teach children their mother tongue and Korea's customs and traditional arts to build individuals' pride in their heritage.

Ethnic pride is publicly demonstrated with museum exhibits, community Korea Day parades and cultural center displays and activities.

---

*Facing page (clockwise from top left): Korean display in the Peabody Museum; Korean-American-published newspapers; a Korea Day parade in New York City; the Korean Association of Chicago; Korean children learning traditional customs in New England; the Korea Liberation Day ceremony in Washington, D.C. Above: gold-gilt Buddha in San Francisco's Asian Art Museum.*

## TREASURES
## OF THE PAST

The cultural heritage of a milleniums-old country was exhibited for the American public during the 1979 through 1981 tour of the "5,000 Years of Korean Art," which appeared in eight cities and exhibited more than 350 Korean art treasures.

The two-year tour included San Francisco, Seattle, Chicago, Cleveland, Boston, New York, Kansas City and Washington, D.C.

Local, national and international media publicized the exhibit and praised the show's variety and excellence. But more apparent from exhibit-goers' and critics' comments and reviews was the "discovery" of traits indigenous to Korean art and culture. They lauded the "splendor" of Korea's "stunning celadon porcelains," "dazzling gold crowns," and "robust and bold" genre paintings.

The show was designed to improve Americans' understanding and appreciation of Korea's rich heritage, as well as its artistic accomplishments.

One writer's comments expressed many viewers' sentiments, "5,000 Years of Korean Art has plenty of dazzlements but it offers, more importantly, a lesson about a remarkable people."

*Facing page: New York City's Metropolitan Museum of Art was one of eight major American museums to host the "5,000 Years of Korean Art" exhibit during its 1979-1981 U.S. tour. Museum patrons viewed art treasures ranging from a circa 3,000 B.C. pot to the elaborate Silla Dynasty gold crowns; (bottom) the show's curators and officials standing outside the banner-draped Met. Above, Minister of Culture and Information Lee Kwang Pyo (center) during opening ceremonies at the Smithsonian Institute, Washington, D.C.*

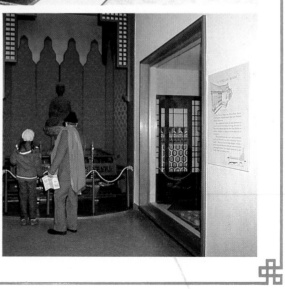

## A HERITAGE PRESERVED

Korean cultural organizations and agencies are improving Americans' understanding and appreciation of one of the world's oldest cultures by expanding their activities outside the Korean-American community.

Korean cultural centers offer historical exhibits, traditional art displays, music and dance performances and study centers promoting Korea's rich cultural heritage. Study classes, seminars and lectures cover all aspects of Korean history, life and philosophy. Major U.S. universities have added Korean sections to their libraries to provide an academic avenue for increasing interest and awareness. And museum displays exhibit Korea's arts and traditional crafts.

*Facing page (clockwise from top left): The Korea Cultural Center in Los Angeles; first director of the center, Lew Chi Ho, receives a certificate of appreciation from L.A. Mayor Thomas Bradley for his "efforts to promote mutual understanding between Korea and the civic community of Los Angeles;" an exhibit of traditional Korean musical instruments at the opening of New York City's Korea Cultural Center; the Korean exhibition at the Smithsonian Institute; Dr. Chang Byong Hae (far left) and staff discuss programs at Seton Hall University's (New Jersey) Asian Bilingual Curriculum Development Center; Yu Tae Hi (right), Miju Hankook newspaper president, presents a Korean dictionary to Dr. Yang Ki Baek, head of the U.S. Library of Congress' Korea Section. Above: The Center for Korean Studies at the University of Hawaii, one of the major centers of its kind in the U.S.*

# MAINTAINING TRADITIONS

Korean-Americans, proud of their rich ethnic background, have preserved the customs and traditions of their homeland—not to comfort the old or homesick, but to nurture the dignity, self-worth and knowledge of their families and community.

*Facing page: (top) Performance of traditional Korean music in New York City and (bottom) the Kwanumsa Buddhist Temple in Los Angeles. This page (clockwise from right): A Buddhist priest and his congregation at the Wonkaksa Buddhist Temple in New York; women making traditional Korean rice cakes in Flushing, New York; Taekwondo master Nam Tae Hi instructing a class in Chicago; Korean children bowing to elders during a lunar New Year's Day ceremony; and Korean-American children learn about their heritage in a native language class.*

## SOME PROMINENT KOREAN-AMERICANS

"Among minority groups in the United States," according to Professor Choy Bong Youn, author of "Koreans in America," "Koreans rank proportionately high in the intellectual and professional fields. This is an especially noteworthy accomplishment for the early immigrants from relatively modest social backgrounds. It is also an indication of the intelligence and perseverance of the Korean-born students who have distinguished themselves as scholars and professionals in America's competitive academic and business worlds.

Korean-Americans have become a recognizable, although proportionately small, ethnic minority in the United States, not by the headlines they have created on the front pages of national papers but by the consistent and progressive personal and community improvements they have made.

Korean contributions, present in almost every field of American endeavor have been especially noticeable in literature, law, medicine, entertainment and the highly competitive business fields.

Consider, for example, the case of the world-renowned Chung family trio—Myung Wha, the cellist; Kyung Wha, the violinist; and Myung Hun, the pianist-conductor. Their extraordinary virtuosity and perfectionism have received critical acclaim throughout the world.

Or the case of the two famous Hyun brothers, Dr. Bong H. Hyun, a highly respected clinical pathologist and author of a hematology textbook used in institutions throughout the world, and his younger brother, Peter, well-known on both sides of the Atlantic and Asia as well, as a multilingual editor and journalist.

Koreans have also earned fame for their theories and inventions, as is the case of Dr. Rho Joon Hui, who developed a biochemical analyzer used on NASA's Apollo flights, and Paik Nam June, who created the first video art exhibition.

Although it is impossible to mention every Korean-American who has made contributions to American culture, or has in some other way become noteworthy, it is important to look at some of the successful people who make up about .3 percent of the U.S. population.

According to David Hsin Fu, author of "Asian American Heritage," "at present the three most well-known names in Asian-American fiction are Korean-born Americans." He refers to Kang Young Hill, Richard Kim and Kim Yong Ik. All came to the United States as students and became naturalized citizens.

## Kang Young Hill

"The late professor Kang was the best known Korean writer," claims Professor Choy Youn Bang. He landed in San Francisco when he was 18 years old, shortly before the Oriental Exclusion Law was passed.

Kang was a top student, but he was especially gifted in literature and poetry. He became the first Korean-born professor of comparative literature at New York University and later worked with the Metropolitan Museum of Art and Encyclopedia Britannica.

Above all, Kang was a gifted writer. His first book, an autobiography called "The Grass Roof," brought him fame as a Korean-American writer. This success was followed by his second book, "East Goes West," and then by a third, "The Happy Grove."

Kang was also considered one of the world's top classical Asian scholars. The late Pearl S. Buck wrote; "Kang Young Hill, distinguished author and lecturer, is one of the most brilliant minds of the East..." During his career, Professor Kang received the Guggenheim Award in creative literature as well as several European prizes for his three novels.

## Kim Yong Ik

Kim Yong Ik is one of history's most famous Korean-American writers. His short stories have been published and republished in international magazines, anthologies and textbooks. His novels have won critical acclaim and two stories have been made into major films in Korea.

*Kim talks with students in his fiction class at Duquesne.*

Six novels bear his name including "The Blue in the Seed" which was placed on the honor list in the 1967 Austrian State Prize and is excerpted in a Danish textbook. "The Happy Days" was selected by the American Library Association as a Notable Children's Book for 1960 and West Germany's Best Youth Book for 1965. Twice his stories were included in Martha Foley's "Best American Short Stories."

Occasionally he also writes for Korean publications and receives packages of squid, kelp, bracken shoots and ginseng in payment. "When I open the packages, I get the most wonderful sensation. I can smell my hometown seafront . . . I can smell the Korean earth. Then I hear my own laughter . . . and sighs."

Kim was born in the southern coastal city of Choong Moo. He attended high school in Seoul and studied in Japanese and American universities. In 1957 he returned to Korea to teach at Korea and Ehwa Universities and reentered the U.S. in the mid-sixties to instruct at various universities. Currently he teaches fiction at Duquesne University in Pittsburgh.

## Richard E. Kim

Richard E. Kim is one of the most accomplished Korean-American novelists. He has written three major novels—"The Martyred," "The Innocent" and "Lost Names." All three books refer to the oppression and exploitation of Koreans by the Japanese during their domination of Korea.

Born in northern Korea, he served as a

liaison officer between the American and South Korean forces during the Korean War. Kim received degrees from both Johns Hopkins University and Harvard and served as assistant professor of English at the University of Massachusetts and professor of English at San Diego State University.

"The Martyred" is the story of the "conflict of the souls of men" during the Korean War. It reached the final round of nominations for the National Book Award the year it was published. For "The Innocent" and "Lost Names," Professor Kim earned the University of Iowa Writers' Workshop Fellowship, the Ford Foundation Foreign Area Fellowship and the Guggenheim Foundation Fellowship.

The New York Herald Tribune described Kim as "one of the ablest young novelists to appear in any nation in decades." The Los Angeles Times said "Richard Kim's brilliant and powerful novels deserve to be included in the small group of 20th-century novels which may be called great."

## A KOREAN-AMERICAN SAGA   By Peter Hyun

On the eve of the centenary of the opening of the "Hermit Kingdom" to the United States, I find it hard to resist the temptation, if not the tenacity, to compare this historic event to my own often stormy but essentially fruitful relationship with Uncle Sam.

In the fall of 1948, as an 18-year-old penniless refugee from North Korea, I found myself aboard a U.S. troopship bound for San Francisco, with a dirty old handbag under my arm and a torn paperback edition of Walt Whitman's "The Leaves of Grass" in my otherwise virtually empty pocket.

Buoyed by my brief shipboard romance with a 17-year-old redhead from St. Joseph, Missouri, I was determined to find the democratic vision of America so powerfully sung by Whitman—and not Hollywood's celluloid version of cowboys and Indians, bang-bang, kiss-kiss, and super cars and super homes.

Upon my landing at the port of disembarkation, I was shocked beyond words to find an unofficial welcome committee consisting of hobos and winos in rags soliciting handouts, and sharp-talking shysters peddling "girls and hot spots."

The worst was yet to come. At a Presbyterian college in the Midwest, where I was to receive a four-year liberal arts education, they tried to ram a highly orthodox version of Calvinism down my throat. When I objected to a theology professor's claim that "the Bible is the greatest literature ever written," I flunked the course and was eventually asked to leave the campus "within forty-eight hours for conduct unbecoming  the son  of a Presbyterian minister from Korea."

My eldest brother, a theology graduate student, wired money so I could join him in New York. During my four-day bus trip, I now recall vividly, I could not help but compare this shattering experience with the USS General Sherman incident, wherein the United States exercised

its gun-boat diplomacy at the turn of the century to try to force the long isolated Korean kingdom to open its door to the West on its own terms.

Indirectly, at least, the Sherman incident benefited Koreans in the sense that the long dormant Korea awoke overnight from its slumber. By the same token, my unexpected expulsion from a Midwestern college induced me to face "the facts of life," American-style.

As if that was not enough, after my few years of flirtation with American University in Washington, D.C. and Columbia in New York, I was deported from the United States in the summer of 1952, thus becoming one of the first victims of the infamous Walter-MacCarren Act, which stipulated, among other things, that the U.S. Justice Department had the right to deport aliens without having to disclose the reason or reasons.

As a student of the Whitmanian Americana, I suddenly felt betrayed—the way my forebearers must have felt when in 1905 U.S. President Theodore Roosevelt recognized Japan's domination of the Korean peninsula in return for the Japanese acceptance of the American occupation of the Philippines.

Having thus ended up in Paris, I began my life as a freelance writer and translator of Korean poetry into English and French. During my 10-year sojourn in Paris and London, I had a series of love affairs with young ladies from various European countries and America.

Strangely enough, my longest and most serious affair was with an American girl, who happened to be one of Teddy Roosevelt's granddaughters. And it was this literary-minded friend from Oyster Bay, Long Island, who, together with poet Stephen Spender, helped me launch my literary career in Europe. To me, at least, her help was like a personalized U.S. grant to a Korean in need.

In the mid-1950s, I was denounced by the Syngman Rhee regime as a Communist. My crime: occasional contributions to liberal journals in Paris, London and Warsaw. During the Chang Myon regime, I became the first Korean cultural attache in Europe. When Gen. Park Chung Hee and his military revolutionaries took over the reins of the government in 1961, however, I lost my job without any warning or severance pay.

By this time, I had a pregnant wife—the niece of Louis Douglas, President Truman's treasury secretary and ambassador to the Court of St. James —whose family had disowned her when we married. Because I could not find a suitable job in Paris or London, my wife and I decided to move to New York.

To make this long story short, it finally took the late Senator Estes Kefauver's special congressional bill to permit me to return to the United States in the summer of 1962. Only in America, I thought, can this happen. For, several months previously, my English friend Anthony Crosland—who later became Britain's foreign secretary and died of a heart attack while in office—had failed to persuade his Conservative colleagues, who were then in power, to grant me a resident permit in England.

In New York, I was lucky enough to find a job as a special correspondent of the New York Herald Tribune. Lucky, because I was able to visit Korea for the first time in 18 years in connection with my assignment to cover the Korean presidential election of 1963.

Eventually, I was asked to join one of America's leading publishers, Doubleday, as a senior editor. In addition to editing children's books, I often went to Europe, both Western and Eastern, to sell the rights to our books there and to acquire the rights to publish suitable European books in the U.S.

In my spare time, I wrote a number of books and articles for major magazines and newspapers in New York, London, Paris and Tokyo. Our two children were now enrolled in a private French school in New York. We bought an old farmhouse in the hills of Kent, Connecticut, where we spent most of our weekends.

When my wife came down with terminal cancer in 1970, two American friends of mine practically forced me to accept their blank checks, to the chagrin of their accountants, with the proviso that I repay them with no interest at my convenience. While my wife's own family did not come to our aid, my friends' generosity was very touching, indeed.

After six years of widowerhood, I married again—this time to a Korean. Now that our two older children are at Tufts and Yale Universities, respectively, my wife, our youngest son and I divide our time between New York and Seoul. And we feel quite at home in both places.

By no means do we represent even a fraction of the Koreans who have found a niche in American society. There are hundreds and thousands of "early settlers" like ourselves, all of whom feel at home in their adopted land; and every year, untold Korean families and individuals immigrate to the "land of the free, and home of the brave."

With its vast land and its rich resources, with its ever-expandable free economic system, America can and does adeptly absorb those determined immigrants eager to work hard and better their lot. With their inborn pride and confidence, with their intelligence and work ethics, they readily become the champions of the U.S.-Korea partnership, thus enhancing the century-old trans-Pacific ties.

## THE ALL-AMERICAN SUCCESS STORY
## OF PHILIP HWANG*

When Kyupin Philip Hwang and his wife, Gemma, both natives of Korea, were students at Utah State University in the 1960s, they labored summers at the Nevada Lodge, a Lake Tahoe casino, to earn money for the school year. Philip worked his way up from dishwasher to busboy to waiter, while his wife packed rolls of coins—often until her fingers bled. Ever optimistic, Phil promised himself that one day he would return to the casino as a guest.

This spring, Philip finally kept his promise. When he took Gemma back to catch the Easter show at the Nevada Lodge, he did so as the owner of a Silicon Valley enterprise that has revolutionized one part of the electronics industry and might be worth $100 million or so if Hwang chose to take it public.

Hwang's specialty is building cathode-ray terminals (CRTs), those now familiar office artifacts that look like TV sets equipped with typewriter keyboards. Through clever manufacturing techniques and application of the latest semi-conductor technology, Hwang's Tele Video Systems Inc. of Sunnyvale, California, has surged to the forefront in this highly competitive field and sales in 1981 exceeded $35 million.

*Tele Video's CRT production plant in the Silicon Valley.*

In 1975, Hwang decided to use the family savings, a modest $9,000, to go into business making electronic games. He set up shop in the proverbial Silicon Valley garage, but couldn't afford to buy monitors. Then Hwang had the bright idea of flying to his homeland, where he made the rounds asking seven Korean TV companies to make

*Philip and Gemma Hwang*

monitors for him. Six turned him down; the seventh said it might be interested—if he could order more than the 200 to 300 monitors a month he had in mind.

Back in California, the indefatigable Hwang approached Atari and other established game manufacturers. When he showed them a sample monitor and quoted a price, they were immediately interested. He was off to Korea again to ask the manufacturer to make 5,000 monitors a month. By this time, Hwang had decided to drop electronic games and concentrate on monitors.

Once he got it going, Hwang's trade was lucrative: he cleared $200,000 within two years. But with new competitors entering the business, he decided to switch to the related field of CRTs.

About six months ago Tele Video moved into first place among independent suppliers of smart terminals.

Rich or poor, the Hwang household is still an exemplar of frugality. There are some outward accoutrements of success, to be sure, such as his-and-hers Mercedeses and a million-dollar home the Hwangs are building in tony Los Altos Hills. But Hwang seems prouder of the fact that Gemma kept the heating bill to $55 last January while some neighbors' bills ran to $250; she did it by covering all the cracks in the house with plastic and turning down the thermostat. Gemma still works part-time at the hospital.

Hwang says his incentive is not to get rich—which in any case he already is—but to build Tele Video into a major corporation. He thinks the company's new series of small business computers will carry Tele Video to $500 million in sales in the next five years.

Whether Tele Video repeats its success or not, the CRT business will never be the same—thanks to Phil Hwang. "Enterprise, challenge, improvement make this a great country," he says. "I like that."

\* Condensed from "Fortune" Magazine.

### Johnny Yune

A successful comedian, Korean-American Johnny Yune has appeared on many television programs, including Johnny Carson's "Tonight Show." He also starred in a comedy movie, "They Call Me Bruce" (below).

## Philip Ahn

Philip Ahn, eldest son of Korean patriot Ahn Chang Ho, was a renowned Hollywood actor who performed in movies before and during World War II. He is probably best known for his role in the TV series, "Kung Fu."

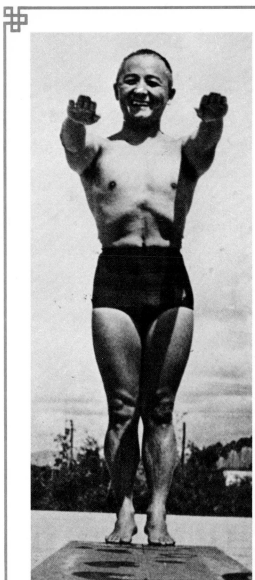

## Sammy Lee

A Korean-American who literally dove into international limelight, Sammy Lee became the first Asian to win two gold medals in the Olympic Games diving competition.

Lee, now a physician in Santa Anna, California, studied medicine at the University of Southern California before joining the U.S. Army Medical Corps in 1942. In 1948 he earned a berth on the U.S. Olympic Team, and then in the 1948 London Olympic games, won a gold medal for diving. He repeated the feat in the 1952 Olympics at Helsinki.

Still active in the sports world after his discharge from the army, Lee was selected by President Dwight D. Eisenhower as one of three presidential representatives to the 1956 Olympic Games in Melbourne. Lee was the first non-white athlete to win the James E. Sullivan Award as the outstanding American sportsman in 1958. Dr. Lee is currently a member of the President's Council on Physical Fitness.

*Facing page (clockwise from top left): Highlighting his illustrious career Lee poses "on the board;" as an army major (with his Sullivan Award trophy); in the Army Medical Corps; on the winners' platform awaiting his first Olympic gold medal; as diving coach; attending an athletic event with President Eisenhower and other dignitaries.*

## The Chung Trio

The most successful Korean-American musical family, sisters Myung Wha, Kyung Wha and brother Chung Myung Hun, have earned international acclaim throughout the world with their performances. Myung Wha (above right and facing page) is the protege of world famous cellist Gregor Piatigorsky and has won many international competitions. Kyung Wha is a violinist and is co-winner of the Edgar M. Leventritt International Competition. Myung Hun is an accomplished pianist and currently the deputy conductor of the Los Angeles Symphony Orchestra.

### Han Nong (Ki Suk)

Internationally acclaimed artist, Han Ki Suk, known professionally as Nong, now operates a gallery in San Francisco.

With no formal art training, Nong began with one-man exhibitions in 1965 and has since toured the U.S., Korea, Taiwan, France, India and Japan. Much of his work is displayed in major galleries worldwide and he is praised for his combination of traditional Oriental and modern techniques.

*Nong (below) stands in front of his San Francisco gallery. Facing page: Nong at work and one of his paintings on display in the New Otani Hotel in Los Angeles.*

## Paik Nam June

Acclaimed as "the world's greatest living legend in the video field," Paik Nam June has been a key figure in video art and technology for 20 years.

The Korean immigrant has gained widespread recognition for his interpretations of life through the use of video art.

Paik left South Korea to earn a degree in Aesthetics from Tokyo University, and in the late 1950s traveled to Germany to study philosophy and contemporary music. After

*Paik Nam June in his video studio preparing for a one-man exhibition at New York's Whitney Museum.*

graduation he experimented in electronic music as an avant garde musician before turning to video as a performer, inventor and artist. In 1963 Paik held the world's first known video exhibition in Germany.

A technical, as well as creative, expert in video art, his electronic techniques have been used by many now entering the field.

A recognized pioneer in this revolutionary electronic art, his best known video work, "Global Groove," debuted in 1973. In 1982, New York's Whitney Museum opened a show devoted entirely to Paik, the first of its kind exhibiting a single video artist's work.

He has received many grants and was recently selected as a consultant to the Rockefeller Foundation.

## Ahn Hyong Nam

Incorporating technology and art, Ahn Hyong Nam pioneered "time art" in the U.S. His 54-foot-high, ever-changing sculpture (top center and right), "Living Lantern of Chicago," was dedicated to the city of Chicago and sits in front of McCormick Place-Donnelly Hall. Another work (bottom), "Light Installation in Space," is displayed at Chicago's Museum of Contemporary Art.

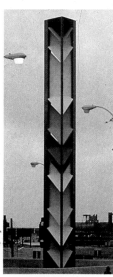

## Kim Keung Sook

An American beauty with Oriental charm, Kim Keung Sook became the first Korean woman to win an official beauty pageant in the U.S. when she was crowned Miss Wisconsin in 1980. She went on to place in the top 10 of the 1981 Miss America Pageant. Kim is a student at the University of Chicago and hopes to become a lawyer.

*Facing page: Kim Keung Sook at the Miss America Pageant and on tour as Miss Wisconsin.*

## Dr. Hyun Bong Hak

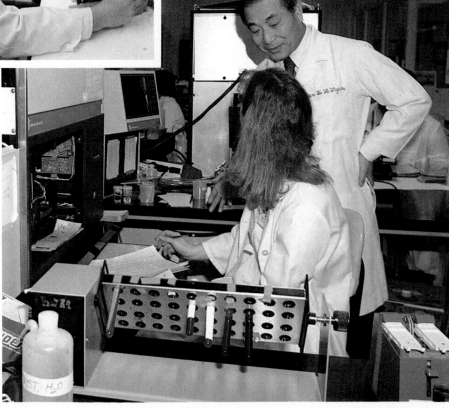

Dr. Hyun Bong Hak, pathologist, is director of the Clinical Laboratory Muhlenburg Hospital and chairman of the Philip Jaisohn Memorial Foundation, New Jersey. As founder of the Korean Medical Association of the United States, he was instrumental in furthering medical cooperation between Korea and the U.S. Dr. Hyun is also an author of a hematology textbook that is widely used in many American medical colleges and hospitals.

## Dr. Joseph C. Kim

Dr. Joseph C. Kim, a renowned ophthalmologist and lecturer at Harvard University Medical School (right), once treated former Korean president Choi Kyu Ha. A specialist in eye diseases and abnormalities he is shown below performing a cataract operation.

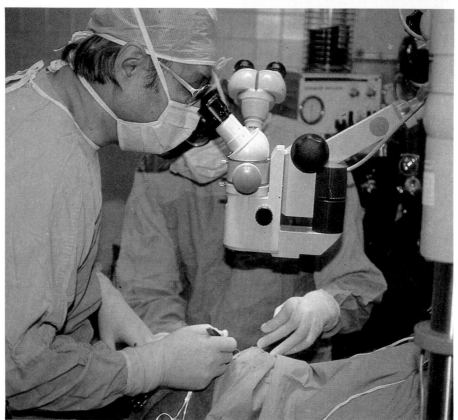

## Dr. Jung Koo Young

Cardiologist Dr. Jung Koo Young, professor of medicine and director of the Heart Station at Thomas Jefferson University Hospital in Philadelphia, is a world-recognized heart authority.

He has written more than 40 books and hundreds of articles about the heart and heart disease. His many works have been translated into eight languages, including Korean, and his textbooks are used extensively in medical schools around the world.

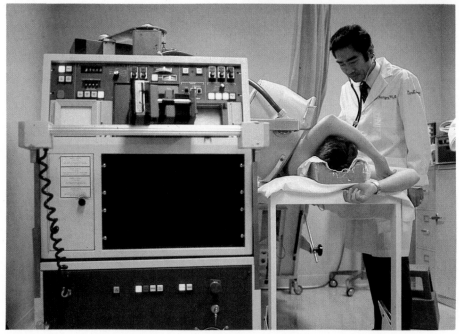

## Dr. Suh Dae Sook

One of the most active leaders in preserving and promoting Korean-American ethnic identity is Suh Dae Sook, director of the Center for Korean Studies at the University of Hawaii.

The center was the first of its kind in the U.S. and he is actively working to expand its scope and activities. Dr. Suh also wrote the two-volume book, "The Korean Communist Movement, 1919-1948."

## Dr. Joon H. Rho

Dr. Joon H. Rho is a professor at the University of Southern California School of Medicine. A bio-chemist for 13 years with the Jet Propulsion Lab, Pasadena, California, he invented an instrument (top left) to automatically analyze bio-chemical activities of the Apollo crews.

## Dr. Suh Nam Pyo

World-renowned scientist Suh Nam Pyo currently holds a full professorship with tenure in mechanical engineering at the Massachussetts Institute of Technology (M.I.T.) and is the director of the institute's laboratory for manufacturing and productivity.

His scientific accomplishments in mechanical engineering include the development of advanced cutting tools and formation of the delamination theory of wear. A theorist as well, he introduced many axioms for design, manufacturing and electro-mechanical hybridizing.

*Dr. Suh in his office (left) and with a student in the engineering laboratory (below).*

### Ahn Phil Young and Susan Ahn

Ahn Phil Young and Susan Ahn, son and daughter of Korean independence fighter, Ahn Chang Ho, now own and operate a Chinese restaurant in a Los Angeles suburb. Susan was the first Oriental woman to become a U.S. navy officer during World War II. Another son of Ahn Chang Ho was the late actor Philip Ahn.

## Dr. Koh Kwang Lim and Chun He Sung

Political science professor and director of the Center for International and Area Studies at Central Connecticut State College, Dr. Koh Kwang Lim and his wife, Chun He Sung, have been praised for their efforts in improving American understanding of Korea through scho-

lastic activities. Chun (Mrs. Koh) is director of research and development at the Human Relations Area File, an inter-university, inter-cultural research organization headquartered at Yale. In 1981 Central Connecticut State College named a scholarship fund for the Kohs in honor of their devotion to international understanding. The scholarship is for students majoring in Korean studies.

*Dr. Koh (above center) and his wife talk with students. Top left, Mrs. Koh at work.*

## Whang Chae Kyong

Andrew C.K. Whang (Whang Chae Kyong), a retired Korean church minister in Washington, was an announcer and commentator for Voice of America (VOA) for 25 years. To many Koreans he is also well-known as an excellent performer of "saw" music. He has appeared in more than 1700 musical performances.

## Yoon Moon Sang

In less than 14 years Yoon Moon Sang built his Amokorn Corporation into an $80 million business with seven subsidiaries.

Yoon, who cites honesty as his secret to success, founded the company in 1968 to produce steel products such as car parts, bearings, and pipes.

Dr. Park Kyung Yun
Remote Sensing Expert
NASA

Dr. Hwang Se Min
Research Scientist
U.S. Navy

Dr. Sung Nak Ho, associate professor of chemical engineering at Tufts University; and his wife Dr. Sung Chong Sook, associate professor of material science at Massachusetts Institute of Technology (MIT).

Dr. Baag Czango
Geophysicist
Exxon Research Dept.

Dr. Kim Kyong Il
Professor of Architectural Design
Harvard University

Dr. Chung Seon Jong
Research Engineer
Ford Aerospace & Communications

Dr. Chun Sung Il
Professor of Business
New Orleans University

Dr. Kim Jong Han
Professor of International Politics
College of William and Mary

Dr. Lee Che Jin
Professor of Political Science
University of Kansas

Dr. Park Han Shik
Professor of Political Science
University of Georgia

Dr. Kim Young Chin
Professor of Political Science
George Washington University

Dr. Joseph M. Ha
Professor of International Politics
Lewis & Clark College

Dr. Kihl Young Whan
Professor of Political Science
Iowa State University

Dr. Koh Byoung Chul
Professor of Political Science
University of Illinois

Dr. Park Sung Bae
Professor of Religion
State University of New York

Dr. Kyo R. Chin
Director of Special Projects
U.S. Dept. of Education

Dr. Son Sung Won
President
St. Cloud State University

Dr. Daniel K. D. Paik
Advisor, Community Network,
L. A. Unified School District

Dr. Yu Eui Young
Director of the Center for Korean
Studies, California University

H. Edward Kim
Sen. Asst. Editor/Photographer
National Geographic

Samuel Ku (Ku Sam Yol)
Reporter
Associated Press

K.W. Lee, Investigative Reporter for the Sacramento Union,
and Editor of "Koreatown."

*Lucuis Foote*

*H. G. Appenzeller*

*Horace Underwood*

*Horace Allen*

*Walter Townsend*

*Mary Scranton*

*William Rockhill*

*The first U.S. legation to Korea.*

# AMERICAN INFLUENCE

## FIRST ENCOUNTERS

he signing of the first treaty between the U.S. and Korea prompted a stream of American travelers and pioneers who would leave a lasting impression on Korea's social framework.

At the head of the procession, at least in terms of rank, was the first American envoy to Korea, Lucius H. Foote, a "reliable and adaptable" career diplomat. He won King Kojong's confidence during his 1883 to 1885 assignment and reinforced the Korean conviction in his country's friendship.

Dr. Horace N. Allen was the first American missionary and physician in Korea. He too gained the king's trust by saving the life of Queen Min's nephew and the first Korean emissary to America, who was gravely wounded in an assassination attempt. Because of his continued friendship with the king, Allen and his fellow missionaries were allowed to openly engage in religious, medical and educational activities. He also used the king's favor to gain approval for business concessions after he shed his religious pursuits. Twice the doctor served as the U.S. envoy to Korea, once to fill the gap between

Foote's departure and William Rockhill's arrival at the U.S. legation in 1883, and a second time after the turn of the century when he held the post for five years.

Other missionary arrivals in the 1880s included Horace G. Underwood and Henry G. Appenzeller who

*American residents in Korea during the 1880s.*

*Students during an exercise class at Korea's first school for women.*

landed together at Inchon (then called Chemulpo) on Easter Sunday, 1885.

Underwood assisted Allen for a time in the latter's hospital and later taught chemistry and physics. Appenzeller, who after two years was able to deliver sermons in Korean, opened the first missionary high school in 1885. Underwood also mastered the language and published the first Korean-English and English-Korean dictionaries in 1890.

Mary Scranton founded Korea's first school for girls. Until her "Girls' School and Home" opened in 1886, Korean women could not enter academic institutions. One Korean writer commented that "if Christian missionaries did nothing else in Korea, the introduction of women's education alone deserves our lasting gratitude."

In the northern part of the kingdom, it was Samuel Moffet who introduced Christianity to the Korean population. Based in Pyongyang, he also became the first moderator for the Presbyterian Church of Korea and actively supported the Korean independence movement until his expulsion in 1936.

The first American businessman in Korea was Walter Townsend, who established a trading company in 1884 at Inchon. He dealt in everything from rice and rubber shoes to

*A garden party at the U.S. legation residence in the early 1900s.*

kerosene and dynamite.

Americans built the first electrical power plant in a joint venture with the royal family in 1898 and over the next two years installed the first telephone system, water works and tram cars. By 1900, Seoul streets were also illuminated by electric, not gas, lights installed by a U.S. company.

*Korea's first modern newspaper.*

Americans' enthusiasm for athletics fostered Koreans' own penchant for Western sports with the introduction of basketball, volleyball and baseball. Now a national pastime with a professional league, Korea's first baseball game was played in 1906. Korea's first modern newspaper, "The Independent," was published by So Chae Pil, a naturalized U.S. citizen. The bilingual paper also carried Korea's first commercial advertising.

A missionary who became politically involved in Korea's struggle for independence was Homer Hulbert. He was given a secret mandate by King Kojong to attend the Hague Peace Conference in 1907 and appealed for Korean autonomy. His plea failed and both he and Allen were expelled by the Japanese because of their overt opposition to Japanese annexation. Hulbert, who once wrote, "I would rather be

*Pioneer missionary Samuel Moffet with Korean Christian women at a 1907 revival meeting in Pyongyang.*

buried in Korea than in West-
minster Abbey," was invited back
by friend and President of Korea,
Syngman Rhee. In his eighties,
Hulbert died on arrival and was buried, true to his wish, in Korea at
Seoul's Foreigners' Cemetery.

Japanese expulsion of the last missionaries in the 1920s and
1930s, because they supported the independence movement and op-
posed Shinto rites in the schools, ended direct American involvement
in Korea until the end of World War II.

During the Korean War some descendants of the original missionaries returned. Richard Underwood acted as an interpreter at the
Panmunjom peace talks and his older brother, Horace, as a naval gun-
nery officer, had the unusual task of directing a battleship's 16-inch
guns on an enemy command post headquartered in his own home
at Yonhi-dong.

Dr. Paul Crane, a second-generation missionary, served as a navy
physician during the war and later as an interpreter for President
Johnson's visit to Seoul and President Park Chung Hee's trip to the
United States.

The early American residents left a legacy of modern thought
and methods which continue to influence Korea's social, economic and
political development.

*Facing page (clockwise from top left): Inchon (then known as
Chemulpo) became a major port following the conclusion of trade
agreements with the United States and other Western nations; a Yi
Dynasty telephone switchboard operator; a baseball game at a Seoul
high school in 1910; Korea's first locomotive, introduced by
Americans. Above: the American-built Hansung Electric Company,
Korea's first electrical power plant.*

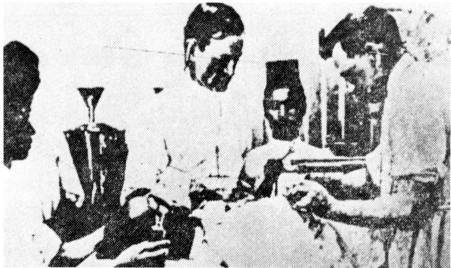

*Facing page: The first Korean-language Bible translated in 1897. Above (top to bottom): The first Western-style hospital; early missionary surgeons introduced Western medical practices; the YMCA in the late Yi Dynasty.*

## THE MISSIONARY PRESENCE

Early American missionaries brought more than just evangelism and a concern for the next world to the Korean peninsula. They introduced Western-style education. Missionary seminaries soon turned into liberal arts colleges and several today have become giant universities.

They also brought Western medical practices and a concern for hygiene and sanitation. Missionaries set up medical schools to train Korean physicians and hospitals for them to practice in.

Less tangibly, but even more important, missionaries brought with them Western values of humanism, individual rights, representative government, primacy of law and a host of other concepts unknown in a Confucian society—concepts unwelcome to the Japanese who were gradually taking control of Korea before their outright annexation in 1910.

The missionaries' schools spawned many of Korea's modern leaders. Moreover, social work in Korea began with the YMCA and YWCA movements inaugurated by missionaries, the latter also taking the lead in the difficult and never-quite-complete emancipation of women.

In their 55 years of activities, the missionaries exerted a strong and continuing influence that endured Japanese suppression and persisted beyond the last missionary's expulsion in 1939. An influence that would become embodied in the foundation of an independent Korea, whose establishment—under a Methodist president—they applauded so fervently.

Edward B. Adams

Julia Lee

Richard R. Underwood

Carl Miller

## SOME
## AMERICAN 'ROOTS'

Thousands of Americans live in Korea today but only a handful of them can trace their "roots" in Korea back decades—some nearly a century.

Richard R. Underwood and Edward Adams have followed their fathers' fathers' footsteps and devoted much of their lives to Korea. Coincidentally, both head

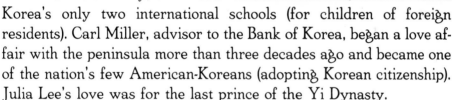

Korea's only two international schools (for children of foreign residents). Carl Miller, advisor to the Bank of Korea, began a love affair with the peninsula more than three decades ago and became one of the nation's few American-Koreans (adopting Korean citizenship). Julia Lee's love was for the last prince of the Yi Dynasty.

In an almost story book romance, Julia Mullock met Yi Ku while they both worked for a New York City architectural firm. She and the M.I.T.-educated prince wed in 1958.

They moved to Korea to join Yi's parents and live in the royal residence, Naksonjae, in Seoul.

The couple had no children of their own and adopted a Korean orphan girl, Un Suk, who is studying in the U.S. At Naksonjae, Julia teaches sewing to handicapped Korean girls and devotes much of her time to welfare projects.

She reminisced about her arrival in Korea 18 years ago, "I was deeply impressed when I first saw Naksonjae in 1963 because of its traditional beauty, along with all the surroundings in Seoul."

Her impressions grew into a lifetime commitment to Korea and its people, as it has for many long-term American residents. "Living in Korea more than 18 years, I really became a genuine Korean, I think."

## FRIENDS

Korean-American friendship has spread to the very roots of both nations. The most rapid growth has come about in the last four years since the Friendship Force International (FFI) and Korean-American Friendship Association launched their civil exchange program.

According to the Atlanta-based FFI president Wayne Smith, more than 6,300 Koreans and Americans took part in the mutual home visit program since its inception in 1978, and during the centennial year about 1,000 Americans will visit Korea.

*Facing page (from top): A Korean family hosts American guests during a home visit; FFI President Wayne Smith; American children model traditional clothing with their new Korean friends.*
*Above (clockwise from top left): a KAFA/FFI tour memorial ceremony at Pusan's UN Cemetery; a Korean shipyard visit; the 1980 Miss Black America and her troupe in Korea.*

## 'THE BIBLE AND COCA-COLA'

From haberdashery and hymnals to blue jeans and jazz, the American influence has permeated Korean society with broad and sometimes radical results, as graphically illustrated in the following excerpt from "The Bible and Coca-Cola," a translation of an article by Sonn Se Il, first published in a Korean magazine commemorating the American Bicentennial:

"America the Beautiful—Land of the Big PX. Dazzling skyscrapers reaching for the stars. Cities laid out like chessboards, two cars in every garage and chewing gum in every mouth, Vivien Leigh melting into the arms of Clark Gable with wild abandon—these are some of the stereotype fantasies many Koreans conjure up when asked to describe America. Conformity and individualism, contradiction and community: it's the Bible and Coca-Cola...

"Americans realize the gap between the worlds of movie and reality, and watch movies for entertainment and relaxation. However, many Koreans take the movie world as the reality of America, and thus the stereotypes are cemented all the more firmly in their minds.

"American pop music and jazz have probably influenced Koreans more than any other medium of American mass culture. Much to the dismay of older traditional Koreans, fast dancing is becoming a part of the youth culture here.

"Mass culture, a by-product of mass production and consumption, is also breaking traditional Korean customs. It encourages ex-

travagance in a land which lacks natural resources, where frugality has been a virtue, if not always in practice, at least in principle.

"Western music was first introduced into Korea by the missionary use of hymns...(but)...probably Christianity's most significant contribution was the introduction of the ideas of democracy and equality....

"Yet, while Christianity helped further Korean nationalism in some respects, it also worked against it by preaching against customs that were an integral part of Korean culture, such as smoking and drinking, and demanded loyalties that conflicted with Korean custom: the strict observance of the Sabbath and a total rejection of other gods, which clashed with ancestor worship and the deeply-rooted Shamanist belief in spirits....

"Koreans have come to be baffled by exactly what is this creature called an American. Their reaction to him is as contradictory as their image of themselves. The Koreans view the Americans with gratitude and resentment, trust and suspicion, love and hate....

"Both countries are moving into a new era of cooperation which will require a redefinition of their relationship. As America matures and gets more history and experience behind her, she will develop a clearer definition of herself. As Korea passes more rapidly into maturation, she will evolve a new definition of herself as a modern nation with a Korean flair.

"And some fateful day an American magazine will run a cover picture of the Statue of Liberty holding a Bible in one hand and a Coca-Cola in the other. And on that day we Koreans may pine nostalgically for the good old days of the conflicting American image."

# PARTNERS IN PROGRESS

"From a position uncomfortably close to the bottom of the international income scale and without the benefit of significant natural resources," a recent World Bank report pointed out, "Korea embarked on a course of industrial growth that became one of the outstanding success stories in international development."

Since the liberation of Korea from 35 years of Japanese rule at the end of WW II, the United States has played an important role in shaping the developmental patterns of the Korean economy.

Major economic assistance from America and other foreign countries kept post-war Korea afloat and later provided the impetus for the "economic miracle" of the 1960s and 1970s. A miracle which has earned the Republic of Korea a respected place among the world's economic leaders.

Dr. John T. Bennett, president of the Korea Economic Institute of America, reviews the Korean-American economic relationship and its future prospects:

"Contrast today with 1962 when Korea began its economic takeoff. No one then could have predicted the way it has worked out. Nor would one have foreseen the growth in Korea's per capita GNP from $80 to more than $1,700, or that of exports from

*Above: President Chun Doo Hwan receives U.S.-Korea Economic Council President Henry Taylor, Feb. 6, 1982. Facing page: one of many Korean-American joint ventures, the Caltex-Honam oil refinery.*

$50 million to $20.7 billion. Few would have anticipated the end of U.S. aid or the development of an enormous mutually beneficial trade and investment relationship with the U.S."

"Few Americans or Koreans are aware that U.S. economic interests go back to the 19th century, when shortly after diplomatic relations were established, U.S. entrepreneurs developed railroad and mining projects. Undercapitalized, they failed and were taken over by the Japanese.

*America played an integral part in Korea's long road to reconstruction following the Korean War.*

"Had the Japanese lost the Sino-Japanese and Russo-Japanese wars, U.S. economic interests in Korea might have continued to develop. As it was, however, President Theodore Roosevelt tacitly recognized that Korea was in the Japanese sphere of influence as part of the Treaty of Portsmouth negotiations and shortly thereafter withdrew U.S. diplomatic representation.

"The Japanese surrender to American troops in Korea produced the next major contact with the U.S. Relief and rehabilitation proved to be the major economic facet. However, tired of the war, eager to demobilize and fearful of Soviet attacks on Europe, the U.S. soon pulled out most of its forces and drew in its defensive perimeter to exclude Korea ....

"But the North Korean attack in 1950 quickly altered perceptions .... That war proved unforgettably savage and devastating. Having mobilized the Western Alliance, many of whose troops participated, the U.S. became committed to the continued defense of the Republic. Relief and reconstruction dominated U.S. economic activity.

"Reconstruction, however, proved a more ambitious task in Korea than in Western Europe. In many ways it was construction, not reconstruction.

"The job in Korea was harder than in Europe and it would prove still harder in the rest of the underdeveloped world. But starting in 1962, Korea began an unprecedented period of unbroken growth, which did not begin to taper off until 1980. It was a record that was to be seldom matched ....

"America continued economic aid through most of the period. The total amount of economic aid in the period, $7.5 billion, seems like a very large figure. But compared to the total amount of wealth produced in Korea during all those years or invested there, it falls into perspective. It was seed capital from which so much has grown.

"During the period when Korea received U.S. aid, its trade steadily grew, as did its exports to America. U.S. markets proved open and eager to buy the kind of low cost merchandise Korea produced. Early on some complained that Korean exports were destroying American jobs, just as they do today. But American prosperity continued and there were other jobs for those who used to make the things the U.S. began importing. By 1979, the equivalent of 170,000 jobs were created to produce U.S. exports to Korea of $4.2 billion. Those jobs were making the things that Korea could buy with the dollars earned selling to America.

"Trade, though the largest part of the economic relationship, is only part of the story. American technology sales have been important, leading also to sales of American equipment. Finally, of course, American lenders, banks and companies have found Korea an attractive place to lend and both secure and profitable.

139

*Top left: The General Motors-Saehan Motor Co. production line; (top right) Dow Chemical Co.-Korea Pacific Chemical Co. plant; Above: A Westinghouse-Korea Electric Co. nuclear power plant.*

"American banks and investors have become increasingly sophisticated about the Korean economy. The first oil shock with the lower growth rate and deteriorating ratio of debt-service payments to export earnings frightened many who were not aware of the evolution of Korea's economic management system. That system allowed the government to pick high growth targets and set out a consistent set of policies and programs to achieve them.

"The goals were determined by Korea's need to employ its growing labor force and so had to be ambitious—to press the economy to its limits. As the bankers subsequently learned, however, the economy managers could put on the brakes if would-be conditions deteriorated...That lesson has generated much more confidence, and we see today that Korea continues to enjoy lender faith despite the second oil shock and the still more difficult export markets of today.

"Trade will continue to be the dominant dimension of U.S.-Korean economic relations in the coming years.

"Currently U.S.-Korean trading is buffeted by two forces, the world recession and major shifts in demand among industries. Korea would have no trouble supplying additional exports, but the demand for them is not there. It would increase its imports, but the lack of export earnings means it cannot pay cash.

"The effect has been slow growth in U.S.-Korea trade. May recovery be expected? Almost certainly. But the key is U.S. interest rates. "The rest of the world also depends on the recovery of the U.S. economy. U.S. revival should therefore spark the growth of Korean trade with those economies as well.

"With growth, the U.S. and Korean economies can move together into increasingly technical, high value-added, and high wage-paying activities. That has been the trend since 1962 in both countries, and there is no reason it shouldn't continue."

# UNITED WE STAND

## THE WAR IS NOT OVER ...

It has yet to be settled with a peace treaty and, although fighting ceased with the signing of the Armistice Agreement, no political settlement has been resolved. The hostilities, if not open, are still evident as United Nations Command and Republic of Korea armed forces guard against attack along the 155-mile-long demilitarized zone (DMZ) splitting the once unified land into North and South.

But the tension along the DMZ is but the proverbial tip of an iceberg, according to U.S. Secretary of Defense Caspar Weinberger.

"Intelligence specialists in both the Republic of Korea and the United States have monitored and documented a steady buildup of the North Korean forces. North Korea has developed what we believe is the largest commando force in the world: some 100,000 men trained in special warfare techniques with a large fleet of AN-2 light aircraft for mobility—a force clearly devoid of defensive characteristics."

The landmined and barbed wire DMZ marking the last hostile confrontation between North Korea and the United Nations Command may also mark the next.

*Facing page (clockwise from top left): Tension often runs high between U.S. and North Korean guards at the Panmunjom Joint Security Area; guards watching the Joint Security Area; a Military Armistice Commission meeting in progress; guards await the meeting's end. Above: an American MP points out Freedom Bridge, the "Bridge of No Return."*

144

## THE KOREAN WAR

The jagged red line marring Korea's map was created by the United States at the end of World War II to facilitate the surrender of the Japanese, but it soon became a separation marked in blood.

The Soviet-backed North Korean army launched a full scale invasion of the South June 25, 1950. U.S. troops had withdrawn a year earlier and the ill-equipped South Korean internal security force was no match for the war-ready North. Responding to South Korean pleas, America rushed troops to the front lines within days and 15 other UN member nations joined the defense effort.

But war quickly enveloped the nation as UN forces were pushed into a shrinking corner of the peninsula. It took a multi-pronged counterattack, spearheaded by MacArthur's Inchon Landing, to regain UN control of the South and as far North as the Yalu River. But Chinese troops joined the North Koreans to recapture Seoul. A second UN attack reclaimed the capital and forced the communists across the 38th Parallel before fighting stalemated.

The Soviet UN representative requested a ceasefire and peace negotiations commenced in June, 1951. But battles continued until July 27, 1953, after more than three years of hostilities, and negotiations were finalized.

The fighting ended almost where it had begun.

---

*Facing page (clockwise): UN Security Council Meeting in June 1950; an American G.I. is treated after he and the South Korean soldier, being helped up the bank, were wounded near Kumhwa; a foot-weary soldier cools his feet; the U.S. 17th Infantry Regiment reaches Haesanjin near the Chinese border; Inchon landing. Above: Secretary of State John F. Dulles inspects the frontlines.*

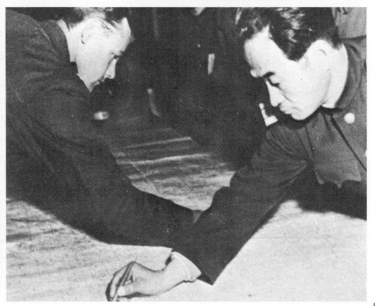

## POST WORLD WAR II 1945-53

The eight years following World War II "is one in which Americans and Koreans came more closely together than ever before," according to University of Southern California history professor, Roger Dingman. "It was then that the contemporary American-Korean relationship was born."

The relationship began when American troops landed in Korea Sept. 7, 1945 to accept the Japanese surrender.

What had been intended as a temporary administrative division of Korea soon became politically permanent. The Soviets claimed "absolute authority" over the North and blocked every move by the U.S. and the United Nations to reunify the country.

Following the May 15, 1948 free elections, control of the South was turned over to the newly-formed Republic of Korea—the only official government in Korea recognized by the UN. The Soviets established their own government in response. Within two years the Soviet-backed North invaded the South and war ravaged the land until 1953.

The signing of the Armistice Agreement marked the end of fighting and the conclusion of a mutual defense treaty which persists to this day.

*Facing Page (clockwise from top left): American occupation troops landing in Korea; Soviet and American troops fraternizing; signing the Japanese surrender in Korea; drawing the DMZ on the Korean map; UN General Assembly debate on the Korean division. Above: General Mark Clark signing the Armistice Agreement in 1953.*

## 'JOINED IN ARMS'

Social and physical scars from the Korean War were still fresh as the Republic of Korea and United States forces hardened the country's defenses against future attacks, strengthening a military alliance that has become one of the world's strongest.

"In no other country . . ." said U.S. Ambassador to Korea Richard L. Walker, "does the United States . . . have as close a daily working relationship as with the armed forces of the host country (Korea)."

The military alliance which was formalized in the 1950s has been shown in exercises, manifested in armed conflict, strengthened by joint exercises and consolidated in formal organizations. Korea and America are bonded by sacrifice and purpose in a relationship which goes beyond guarding the peninsula.

The 1960s were marked by the signing of the Status of Forces Agreement (SOFA) and the dispatch of Korean troops to Vietnam.

In the 1970s the two countries began the free world's largest joint/combined annual exercises, Team Spirit.

In the 1980s the I Corps (ROK/US) Group was renamed the ROK-US Combined Field Army, and joint training programs were expanded. In the 1990s these allies will continue to protect peace on the peninsula.

*Facing page (clockwise from top left): ROK army soldiers in Vietnam; the signing of the Korea-U.S. Status of Forces Agreement (SOFA); the inaugural ceremony of the Korea-U.S. Combined Forces Command (CFC); a Team Spirit exercise. (Above): President Chun Doo Hwan inspects a unit of the Combined Field Army.*

## A MUTUAL COMMITMENT

"Korea is today too important an American partner to be considered as derivative of our relations with any other nation," according to Richard L. Walker, U.S. Ambassador to Korea. "Korea is a special ally which is committed to defending and doing much more than any other ally in terms of sharing the common burden of defense.

"In the past three decades, the U.S. has returned to a recognition of Korea as an allied nation and partner eminently deserving of close attention in and of itself."

In a land rebuilt from the ashes of war, bitter lessons of the past have not been forgotten and neither have proven friends. Both before and during the last 100 years, Korea's security has been justifiable cause for concern. There is no stability in Asia without the balance of military preparedness in Korea.

In 1982, there is unanimous Korean-American agreement that peace, prosperity and security come from remembering the costs and lessons of past wars, and from combined preparations and plans to prevent another.

*Facing page: The first of 24 U.S. Air Force A-10 "Thunderbolt II" close air support aircraft flew into Suwon Air Base March 3, 1982, as part of America's modernizing defense force in Korea. Above: The 14th Session of the Korea-U.S. Security Consultative Meeting March 30-31, 1982. U.S. Defense Secretary Caspar W. Weinberger and Korea Defense Minister Choo Young Bock head the discussions of mutual security concerns.*

"The U.S. continues to take pride in being an integral part of the forces along the DMZ," reasserted U.S. Vice President George Bush during a three-day visit to Korea in spring, 1982.

"Today the ROK and U.S.A. meet each other as equal partners whose mutual interests in peace and freedom have helped insure stability and progress in Northeast Asia," observed U.S. Defense Secretary Caspar Weinberger as he met with his Korean counterpart, National Defense Minister Choo Young Bock, during the 14th Annual ROK-U.S. Security Consultative Meeting in Seoul.

"The Korean people consider the establishment of peace in Korea as the paramount national objective and despite various economic difficulties, have dedicated enormous funds to national defense," Choo told Americans during the conference.

"Historically, Korea has been known to the West as the 'Land of the Morning Calm,' but geographically it has always been an arena for the rivalry of continental and maritime powers in the region and, as such, has constantly engaged the attention of the world. Even at the present moment, it is a place where the danger of war is an ever-present possibility, stronger than anywhere else in the world."

"The U.S. and the Republic of Korea are tied to an eternal bond of friendship and, in Korea, friendship calls for true friends to weep together in sad times, to help each other in difficult times and to share happier times," noted Choo, adding, "We have made our first hopeful step into a second century of friendship."

"One day," predicted Choo, "I believe this friendship will reward us with blessed fruition that people around the globe will be envious of."

*Facing page: Secretary of Defense Caspar W. Weinberger receives a briefing at the DMZ in March 1982. Above: Korean President Chun Doo Hwan (center) meets with Adm. Robert Long, commander-in-chief, U.S. Forces-Pacific and other Korean and American officials. Bottom: ROK Defense Minister Choo Young Bock confers with U.S. Gen. John A. Wickham Jr., commander-in-chief, United Nations Command.*

# THE CENTENNIAL YEAR

## A YEAR OF FRIENDSHIP

The 1982 Korea-U.S. centennial year represents more than the passage of time. It marks a milestone within an era of international friendship. Many American states and cities have proclaimed 1982 as Korean-American Friendship Year and official events and presentations have

demonstrated the enthusiasm shared by the peoples of both nations.

Numerous lectures and symposiums on Korea-U.S. relations were presented to emphasize the historical, political and social significance of the year.

Community presentations, including many special events from parades to exhibitions, featured traditional and popular music, dance and art to emphasize Korea and America's rich cultural attributes. Scholastic and social exchanges further expanded individual and group experience with the contrasting but compatible lifestyles of Korea and America.

Cultural activities in Korea also showed the traditional and modern sides of both countries. U.S. military bands and college choirs presented public musical performances and Korean performers reciprocated with shows at military bases.

All events and activities commemorating the Korean-American centennial year demonstrate a close and growing bond between two peoples joined in history and spirit.

*Facing page: Some of the hundreds of proclamations marking 1982 U.S.-Korea Friendship Year. Above: a friendship centennial tournament between Korea and Yale university tennis teams in Seoul.*

## THE TIES THAT BIND...

In his first visit to the Republic of Korea in April 1982, U.S. Vice President George Bush commemorated the two nations' 100 years of diplomatic relations and friendship. The following are excerpts of his speech to the prime minister of Korea:

"I came to Korea in part to join with you as we celebrate not so much the first 100 years of our friendship, but the next 100 years.

"There is so much that binds us. When Commodore Shufeldt signed our treaty a 100 years ago...both our countries were agrarian economies. Now we are modern, industrial states...In such an age, our ties of trade and investment will grow.

"The nation...thrives on capitalism. Your economy, like ours, is rooted in free enterprise...which reflects the will and diversity of the people.

"The closeness of our ties are reflected in so many ways—in the enormous community of Korean-Americans living in the U.S.; in the 7,000 KATUSA (Korean Augmentation Troops to the U.S. Army) in the U.S. armed forces. In just the last 30 years we have fought in two wars together.

"I met with Korean and American soldiers, the unsung heros of our peace-keeping forces. I can think of no more dramatic example of the unity of our peoples than in those sentinels who keep lonely vigil along that perimeter..."

*Facing page: (top) U.S. Vice President Bush addressing the Korean National Assembly and (bottom) at a ceremony in front of the Korean Capitol Building. Above: Bush with Korean President Chun Doo Hwan.*

## CENTENNIAL ACTIVITIES

*Clockwise from top left: Some of the states and cities presenting 1982 Year of Friendship Proclamations to Korea included: Baltimore, Maryland; the State of Hawaii; New York City, New York; Newport News, Virginia; and Norfolk, Virginia.*

*(Clockwise from top right) Marshall Green gives a lecture on Korean-American relations; Andre Kim fashion show presented at the Yongsan U.S. Army Garrison; Mountain climbing outing with U.S. Ambassador Richard L. Walker, sponsored by the Federation of Korean Industries; and the 1982 Seoul International Marathon.*

# A CENTURY OF NOTE

"The centennial should be a turning point for renewing the mutual commitments of our two countries toward the next century on the basis of maturity and beneficial partnership."

**Lew Byong Hion, Korean Ambassador to the U.S.A.**

"The centennial really marks a progression of increasing American interest about Korea. The future seems to me to dictate that our interchange will expand and will not only be based upon a common strategic purpose but more and more common economic interests."

**Richard Sneider, former U.S. Ambassador to Korea**

"I believe that the centennial celebration is worthwhile in that it underscores the warm and friendly relations that have existed and continue to exist between the people of Korea and people of the United States."

**William P. Rogers, former Secretary of State**

"I believe that we (U.S.-Korea) begin our second century of official diplomatic relations with a remarkably solid basis for friendship and further mutual enrichment."

"I think that it is important that there is a milestone like one hundred years someone has to recognize, in order to deepen our mutual understanding."

**Rear Admiral J.J. Ekelund, Superintendent of the Naval Postgraduate School, Monterey, Oregon**

"We enter our second century of formal state-to-state relations with Korea with ample reason for optimism. Our security cooperation is close, our cultural ties harmonious and our political destinies strongly intertwined."

**Richard L. Walker, U.S. Ambassador to Korea**

"I think both Korea and America can be very proud of the achievements of Korea under difficulties and adversities. To me the future looks bright for Korea."

**Dean Rusk, former Secretary of State**

"I see continuous, strong relationships between Korea and the U.S.A. and I see a continuing and growing and deepening relationship."

**Horace G. Underwood, Founder, Seoul Foreign School**

"The centennial celebration reflects the intentions of the U.S. and Korea to reaffirm its commitment to that goal. Korea has been a long-standing friend of the U.S. and the centennial celebration is an excellent vehicle for highlighting that fact as well."

**Edward I. Koch, Mayor of New York City, New York**

"I believe that any time two nations show concern for others, relations between them will naturally be very positive. The United States and the Republic of Korea are two such nations. Both nations strive to maintain good relations and Korea and the United States have enjoyed a very positive and cooperative alliance."

**Tom Bradley, Mayor of Los Angeles, California**

# THE SECOND CENTURY

he 1982 centenary observance is an opportune time to reflect on past events and achievements which have cemented the strong relationship Korea and America now enjoy. But more important, it is a time to look forward to the second century; its challenges, promises, and responsibilities.

Tomorrow will be the true test of the political and private bonds which have grown and matured during the past 100 years. Dr. Robert Oxman, president of the Asia Society, analyzes Korea and America's future and the strengths and weaknesses which must be nurtured or mended as the nations and their citizenry begin another 100 years.

"Today our two nations interact on almost every level of society. Now the challenge is to look ahead to the next 100 years in which all of us hope that Korea and the United States will continue to join together in a common cause to provide stability and prosperity in the Asia and Pacific region.

"One of the major challenges for the next century is to overcome the gaps in knowledge and information that still divide our full understanding of each other. The first thing that I ever learned about Asia occurred when I was about four years old listening to a nursery rhyme in which I found the way to get to Asia was to begin digging. Since that time, I have recognized that geography and culture create a considerable chasm between us. Now is the time to truly begin digging so that the second century of U.S.-Korea relations can be known as the Century of Understanding.

"What we all need are fresh perspectives on Korea, on the United States, and on our mutual roles in the Asian era in world history, one in which the greatest dynamism and creative energy is going to be

*Today's children are tomorrow's society; they will be the ones to continue Korea and America's bonds of friendship and cooperation.*

found in the countries of the Pacific Basin area. Asia is moving into the center stage of the world's attention. Whatever measurement you use, whether economic growth, trade, education and literacy, cultural creativity or geopolitical concerns, Asia is increasingly dominating the attention of the globe. In this Asian era the United States and Korea both have critical roles. In many ways, Korea is an example of both the dynamism and the danger in the years ahead. The United States will still be a major partner in the age of the Pacific. In this sense both Koreans and Americans have much to contribute to the future of this region and the world.

"There are three dimensions of the period I see ahead which will link together Korea and the United States in the broader Pacific region.

"The first dimension is geopolitics, and here Korea is the classic example as we watch world powers swirl around the Korean Peninsula. In this respect, one can be either a pessimist or an optimist.

"The pessimist can point back and say that we have inherited an ominous history characterized by several wars and ongoing tensions or he can look ahead and say that Asia has the greatest potential for crises along armed borders. Yet even the pessimist must admit there have been new trends which give room for hope. The Republic of Korea is pursuing a policy of openness and a desire for negotiations.

"But if one is an optimist, there is also ample evidence to underscore hopes for a more stable period ahead. The United States enters the decade of the 1980s with a better advantage in the Pacific region. And from a Korean perspective we can see a similar kind of reaching out to new opportunities. Indeed, the emergence of third-party indirect trade between Korea and China is yet another sign of fresh possibilities on the Asian geopolitical stage. Yet the optimist must be careful and recognize that a new era of openness has just begun and border clashes could certainly undercut aspirations for stability.

"The second dimension of the Asian era is of economics, and once again Korea is an important example. Asian countries are indeed in a period of remarkable takeoff in growth and trade. In the past decade, Korea's economy has shown a similar growth, with an annual rate of 8-12% in GNP. Similarly, the ASEAN countries are in a period of takeoff although it is less than their East Asian neighbors. Even the Asian giants, China and India, have begun to move ahead.

"In many ways Korea exemplifies Asia's economic future. It is a future which will have both great growth and considerable problems and which will draw together the countries in the Asia Pacific region in a new kind of international economic web. Above all, it is a future in which economics will be as important as military factors in the security of that part of the world.

"The third dimension of this Asian era takes us inside the countries of the region and focuses on their creative energy. Here again Korea stands as a key example. So often in the past Americans have missed this internal transformation, the story of "inside Asia." The time has come for us to look at Asia not only from the outside in, but also from the inside out. Here I am impressed that many Americans by having deeper encounters with Asians in government and academic communities and in business and banking are in the forefront of the endeavor to understand Asia."

But the progressive actions of the influential but relatively few individuals is only a beginning of the efforts needed to create an era of stability, peace and understanding in the Pacific Basin and between Korea and America. It is similar to the perspective which must be taken during this centennial year—the past events are only preparations for the actions of the future—a future which begins with the second century.

Korea and the United States reaffirm their close bonds daily through political, social, economic and military activities. A symbol of the two nations' relationship overlooks the Pacific Ocean from a hilltop in the Los Angeles Angels Gate Park.

The monument was presented during the U.S. Bicentennial in 1976, in the hope that the bell will "forever sound the continued prosperity of the United States of America and the Republic of Korea, together with the enduring friendship of the two nations, which is sealed by a mutual faith in freedom and independence."

# APPENDIX

# A CHRONOLOGY

## OF KOREAN-AMERICAN RELATIONS

## 1834

May 13    Edmund Roberts, who had explored in the Far East as a
          special agent for the United States, reported to the U.S.
          secretary of state that opening trade with Japan might
          lead to trade with Korea. This was the earliest official
          expression of American interest in Korea.

## 1866

Jan. 11   The American schooner "Surprise" was shipwrecked
          off the Korean coast. The crew was "treated kindly" by
          the Korean authorities and escorted across the Yalu
          River to China.

Rear Admiral John Rodgers, commander of the 1871 American expedition into Korea.

Aug. 20    The "General Sherman," an American merchant schooner seeking to open up trade with Korea, dropped anchor off Pyong-yang. Korean authorities twice sailed toward the vessel, but were frightened off by warning shots fired from the ship. A few days later the "General Sherman" ran aground and the Koreans burned it on Sept. 15.

# 1871

May 19    A five-ship naval expedition from the American Asiatic Fleet under the joint command of Rear Admiral John Rodgers and the American minister to China, Frederick Low, undertook a punitive expedition. A few days later the fleet, including the USS Colorado, anchored off Kanghwa Island and landed a contingent of troops which clashed with the Korean defenders, killing or wounding more than 300. The U.S. force also destroyed five forts. This incident is

The Colorado, flagship for the five-ship expedition that clashed with Korea in 1871.

known as the "Shin-mi Yang-yo" or the 1871 American Incursion.

June 10    The fleet withdrew and sailed back to China, reporting that action was taken to "punish the natives" for the General Sherman attack.

# 1882

| | |
|---|---|
| May 22 | The United States officially established diplomatic relations with Korea when Commodore Robert W. Shufeldt negotiated and signed the Treaty of Peace, Amity, Commerce and Navigation at Chemulpo. The Shufeldt Treaty, ratified one year later, contained an extraterritorial article and established diplomatic and trade relations. |

A copy of the Korea-U.S.A. Treaty of Peace, Amity, Commerce and Navigation.

# 1883

| | |
|---|---|
| May 20 | Lucius H. Foote, the first minister of the United States to Korea, presented his credentials to King Kojong. |
| July 19 | King Kojong sent a special mission to America, |

*Min Yong Ik*

designating Min Yong Ik as minister plenipotentiary and envoy extraordinary and Hong Yong Sik as vice minister of the mission. They and four staff members arrived at San Francisco to study the customs and postal service, public school system, defense systems, arsenals and other U.S. activities and facilities. The mission toured Washington D.C. and New York before returning to Korea May 31, 1884.

# 1888

Jan. 17    Pak Chong Yang presented his credentials as the first resident Korean minister to the United States.

# 1899

Spring    The Korean emperor (the king assumed that title in 1897) requested the United States to initiate an international accord to protect Korea's integrity. American ambassador, Horace N. Allen, on instructions from his government, refused the request.

# 1902

Dec. 22    The first 121 Korean immigrants left Korea to work on Hawaiian sugar plantations.

# 1905

Nov. 24      U.S. Secretary of
War William H.
Taft and Japanese
Prime Minister
Taro Katsura
signed the Taft-
Katsura Memo-
randum in Tokyo,
whereby the

*T. Katsura*          *W.H. Taft*

United States agreed to recognize Japanese sovereignty over Korea in exchange for Japan's promise not
to interfere in the Philippines. The next day the U.S.
announced the withdrawal of its mission from Korea and
declared that it was prepared to deal with Japan from
then on in all matters relating to Korea.

Nov. 28      The U.S. legation in Seoul closed.
Dec. 16      The Korean legation in Washington closed.

# 1908

May 19       The United States and Japan concluded a treaty for the
protection of trademarks and copyrights in Korea.

# 1910

Aug. 29      Japan forcibly annexed the Korean peninsula, putting
Korea under 35 years of Japanese colonial rule.

# 1919

The Little Theater in Philadelphia, site of the First Korea Congress.

| | |
|---|---|
| March 1 | Encouraged by the doctrine of self-determination declared by President Woodrow Wilson at the end of World War I, the Koreans revolted against the Japanese. The Samil (March 1) Independence Movement was brutally suppressed by Japanese forces. |
| April 14-17 | The three-day First Korea Congress, presided over by So Chae Pil (Philip Jaisohn), was held at the Little Theatre (now Plays and Players Theatre) in Philadelphia. Korean independence movement leaders and student delegates in the U.S. attempted to enlist support from world powers for Korea's independence. |

# 1920-1941

Korea's relations with the U.S. were characterized by light trade and missionary activities. Korean imports from the U.S. rose to $3,159,255 in 1922 and dropped to $1,664,948 in 1925. Korean exports to the U.S. averaged only $50,000 annually. Japanese control of the economy and a low demand for American products limited trade expansion. Missionary activities, also hampered by the Japanese occupation force, were completely curtailed in the mid-30s with the expulsion of the remaining missionaries.

# 1941

July       Syngman Rhee, who had been designated chairman of the Korean Commission in Washington by the cabinet ministers of the Korean provisional government, presented a letter to the U.S. secretary of state and credentials of state together with a letter from Kim Ku, executive chief of the provisional government of the Republic of Korea, to President Franklin D. Roosevelt, all dated June 6, 1941. Kim requested restoration of the "diplomatic relations opened between the United States and Korea in 1882."

# 1943

Dec. 1       The Cairo Declaration was issued. This declaration stated that the United States, China and Russia, "mindful of the enslavement of the people of Korea, are determined that in due course Korea shall become free and independent."

# 1945

Feb. 8       U.S. President Roosevelt discussed the question of a trusteeship for Korea with Russian Marshal Stalin during the Yalta Conference. Roosevelt said that he had in mind

*Syngman Rhee and Kim Ku*

**Yalta Conference.**

a trusteeship administered by U.S., Soviet, and Chinese representatives. Stalin also favored a period of trusteeship, but stated that there should be British participation.

June 13    President Truman informed Chiang Kai Shek that the U.S., the Soviet Union and the United Kingdom had agreed upon a four-power trusteeship for Korea.

July 26    The Potsdam Proclamation was issued stating the "terms of the Cairo Declaration shall be carried out," but omitted any time requirements.

Aug. 15    Korea was liberated from Japanese colonial rule when Japan surrendered.

Sept. 7    U.S. military government was established for South Korea in accordance with Proclamation No. 1, issued by General of the Army Douglas MacArthur, commander-in-chief, U.S. Armed Forces, Pacific.

Sept. 8    United States occupation troops entered Korea. Soviet forces entered the North a few weeks earlier.

Dec. 27    Foreign ministers of the U.S., Britain and the Soviet Union, "with a view to the re-establishment of Korea as an independent state," agreed to establish a joint (U.S.-U.S.S.R.) commission in Korea. The commission had representatives of the U.S. command in the South and the Soviet command in the North, to assist in forming a provisional Korean government.

# 1946

March 20      The joint commission held its first meeting in Seoul.

# 1947

May 21      The joint commission reconvened at Seoul.
July 2      The joint commission reached another impasse on the subject of consultation.
Nov. 14      The U.N. General Assembly adopted a U.S.-proposed resolution establishing a nine-nation U.N. Temporary Commission on Korea to assist in expediting fair elections for an independent Korea.

*UN Security Council debates the Korean question.*

# 1948

Jan. 12      The U.N. Temporary Commission on Korea held its first meeting in Seoul after the Soviets barred their entry to the North.

May 10      Korean National Assembly elections were held in the South with observer teams of the U.N. Temporary Commission on Korea overseeing the balloting.

Aug. 15      Formal inauguration of the Republic of Korea government held. U.S. military government in South Korea was terminated and the transfer of authority began.

Korean Cabinet members celebrate UN's validation of the new Korean government.

Aug. 24      President Rhee and U.S. Commander Lt. Gen. John R. Hodge signed an inter-military agreement providing for the transfer of juris-diction over the security forces (including police, constabulary and coast guard) to the new government.

Aug. 26      An American diplomatic mission to Korea was established under the direction of John J. Muccio, special representative of the president to Korea, with the rank of ambassador.

Aug. 26      President Truman announced that the Economic Cooperation Administration would assume the relief and rehabilitation functions in Korea formerly administered by the U.S. Department of the Army.

# 1949

Jan. 1      The U.S. extended de jure recognition to the ROK government.

Feb. 6      The new U.N. Commission on Korea assumed its duties in Seoul.

April 20      John J. Muccio presented to President Rhee his credentials as the first U.S. ambassdor to Korea.

July 1      The U.S. Army Korean Military Advisory Group (KMAG) was established to train the Korean Internal Security Force following the withdrawal of the United States main force from South Korea.

# 1950

| | |
|---|---|
| Jan. 14 | Korea and the U.S. signed a civil aviation agreement on the operation of Kimpo International Airport in Seoul. |
| Jan. 26 | The Korea-U.S. Mutual Defense Agreement was signed and put into effect. |
| June 25 | Korean War erupted. North Korean armed forces launched a full-scale surprise invasion against the Republic of Korea. U.S. President Truman authorized the U.S. commander in the Far East to furnish military supplies to the Republic of Korea. |

*Republic of Korea Marines hoist the Korean flag over Seoul after its recapture Sept. 28, 1950.*

| | |
|---|---|
| July 6 | The first U.S. army unit, "Task Force Smith," deployed to Korea, clashed with the North Korean army near Suwon. |
| July 8 | President Truman, in response to the July 7 U.N. Security Council resolution, named Gen. Douglas MacArthur commander of all U.N. forces in Korea. |

U.S. Army paratroopers dropping into Sunchon to cutoff North Korean retreat.

Sept. 15  Combined Korean and U.S. army and marine forces, led by Gen. MacArthur, landed at Inchon.

Sept. 30  Ground forces of 15 U.N. member nations joined American and South Korean soldiers to fight the North Korean army.

Nov. 5  The U.N. Command in Korea reported that "in certain areas of Korea, the U.N. forces are meeting a new foe, Chinese Communist military units."

Dec. 1  The U.N. General Assembly, by a vote of 51-0-5, adopted a resolution establishing the U.N. Korean Reconstruction Agency to conduct a program of relief and rehabilitation in Korea.

Dec. 14  The U.N. General Assembly, by a vote of 52-5-1, adopted a resolution to establish a group "to determine the basis on which a satisfactory ceasefire in Korea can be arranged."

U.S. Marines on the outskirts of Seoul October 1950.

# 1951

| | |
|---|---|
| April 11 | President Truman relieved General of the Army Douglas MacArthur of his Far East Command and appointed Lt. Gen. Matthew B. Ridgway. |
| July 10-11 | A U.N. Command delegation headed by Vice Adm. C. Turner Joy met twice at Kaesong with a Communist delegation led by Lt. Gen. Nam Il to discuss a cease-fire. |

*Gen. Douglas Macarthur delivering retirement address to Congress.*

| | |
|---|---|
| Oct. 25 | Armistice negotiations in Korea were resumed at a new conference site near Panmunjom. The U.S. agreed, despite South Korean objections, to move the site from Kaesong to Panmunjom, a decision resulting in considerable advantage to the North. |

# 1952

| | |
|---|---|
| May 24 | The Republic of Korea and U.S. governments signed an economic coordination agreement establishing a combined economic board comprising representatives of the Republic of Korea and the U.N. Command. |

Dec. 2-5　　President-elect Dwight D. Eisenhower visited the Korean combat zone as a step to implement his campaign pledge to stop fighting in Korea. During his visit he conferred

*Part of the UN truce delegation at Kaesong (from left): South Korean MG Paik Sun Yup, U.S. Vice Adm. C. Turner and MG Henry Hodges.*

with President Rhee and other Korean officials and American military commanders.

# 1953

April 26　　Plenary sessions of the delegations negotiating an armistice in Korea were resumed at Panmunjom, despite Republic of Korea opposition.

July 27　　The Armistice Agreement was signed at Panmunjom.

Aug. 8　　At the end of talks in Seoul, President Rhee and U.S. Secretary of State John F. Dulles announced that they had initialed a draft Korean-U.S. mutual defense treaty.

Oct. 1　　The Korea-U.S. Mutual Defense Treaty was signed in Washington D.C. by Foreign Minister Y.T. Pyun and Secretary of State Dulles (effective Nov. 17, 1954).

*Signing the Mutual Defense Treaty.*

*Korean President Syngman Rhee with U.S. President Dwight D. Eisenhower and family during Rhee's 1954 visit to the US..*

# 1954

| | |
|---|---|
| July 26 | President Rhee visited America at the invitation of U.S. President Eisenhower. On July 28, Rhee addressed the joint session of the U.S. Congress, warning that "the way to survival is not the way of wishfully hoping for peace when there is no peace ... We must act now." |
| Nov. 17 | Korea and the U.S. initialed an agreement setting forth the broad areas of agreement which existed between the two governments on political, economic and military matters. |

# 1955

| | |
|---|---|
| Sept. 21 | Korea and the U.S. established an investment agreement. |

# 1956

| | |
|---|---|
| March 17 | Secretary of State John Foster Dulles visited Korea for talks with Korean leaders on the unification of Korea. |
| Nov. 28 | Korea and the United States signed a treaty of friendship, commerce and navigation (put in force Nov. 7, 1957). |

# 1957

| | |
|---|---|
| April 24 | The Korea-U.S. Civil Aviation Agreement was signed and put into effect. |

# 1958

| | |
|---|---|
| Jan. 31 | The Korean and U.S. governments concluded a contract to build a fertilizer plant at Naju, Korea. |
| Oct. 27 | The U.S. announced that the U.N. forces would not be withdrawn from Korea until the North Koreans accept free elections Korea-wide. |

# 1959

| | |
|---|---|
| Jan. 9 | President Rhee said Korea could wage a war against the North without U.S. help. |
| Dec. 12 | New U.S. Ambassador McConaughy arrived in Seoul. |

# 1960

| | |
|---|---|
| April 26 | President Syngman Rhee resigned following the April 19 student uprising, and Foreign Minister Huh Chong became head of a caretaker government. |
| June 19 | President Eisenhower arrived in Korea for a visit and addressed a special session of the Korean National Assembly, pledging full U.S. support to the Republic of Korea government in accordance with the Mutual Defense Treaty. |
| Aug. 12 | The Korean National Assembly elected Yun Po Sun as president and approved the appointment of Chang Myun as prime minister a week later. President Eisenhower extended congratulations to President Yun. |
| Aug. 31 | The U.N. Korean Reconstruction Agency (UNKRA) ended its activities. |

# 1961

Feb. 8        Korea and the United States concluded agreements with respect to U.S. economic, technical and related assistance to Korea, superseding previous economic aid agreements.

Nov. 13-17    General Park Chung Hee, who succeeded in his May 16 military revolution, visited Washington D.C. at the invitation of President John F. Kennedy, and discussed plans to transfer power to a civilian government.

# 1962

Sept. 20      Negotiations were resumed between Korea and the United States for a Korea-U.S. Status-of-Forces Agreement (SOFA).

# 1963

Jan. 8        Korea and the U.S. signed a consular convention to regulate consular activities of the two nations.

July 27       The U.S. State Department repledged that American armed forces would remain in Korea until "lasting peace with justice can be attained."

Nov. 26       Korean President-elect Park Chung Hee met with President Lyndon B. Johnson following funeral services for the assassinated President Kennedy. In summit talks, Johnson assured continued U.S. military and economic support to Korea.

Dec. 17       Park Chung Hee was sworn in as chief executive of the new civilian government.

# 1964

Jan. 28    U.S. Secretary of State Rusk visited Korea and assured President Park Chung Hee of continued U.S. aid.

April 10    Prime Minister Choi Tu Son headed a Korean delegation to attend funeral services for Gen. Douglas MacArthur.

*Republic of Korea troops in Vietnam.*

# 1965

Jan. 8    Korea decided at the request of the United States and South Vietnamese governments to dispatch 2,000 non-combat troops to South Vietnam.

May 16-27    President Johnson invited President Park to the U.S. During summit talks, Johnson asked Park to send more Republic of Korea troops to South Vietnam.

*U.S. President Lyndon B. Johnson and Korean President Park Chung Hee.*

# 1966

Jan. 1-2    Vice President Hubert Humphrey visited Korea to ask for Korea's continued military assistance to South Vietnam.

Feb. 22    Vice President Humphrey, accompanied by U.S. Ambassador-at-large W. Averall Harriman, flew into Seoul for a 20-hour unofficial visit to confer with President Park Chung Hee about the Vietnam situation.

*Korean and American officials signing the SOFA agreement.*

July 9    The Korea-U.S. Status-of-Forces Agreement (SO-FA) was signed in Seoul.

Oct. 31    President Johnson visited Korea for summit talks with President Park and thanked Korea for its military support in Vietnam.

# 1967

Oct. 30    The first Korea-U.S. Commerce Ministers meeting was held in Seoul to discuss ways of expanding trade and economic cooperation between the two nations.

Dec. 11    Korea and the U.S. concluded a bilateral cotton textile trade agreement.

# 1968

U.S. President Lyndon B. Johnson addresses the Korean National Assembly.

| | |
|---|---|
| Jan. 21 | A 31-man North Korean commando unit raided Seoul in an assassination attempt against President Park. |
| Jan. 23 | North Koreans seized the U.S. ship Pueblo and its crew off Wonsan. |
| Feb. 11 | U.S. Presidential envoy Cyrus Vance arrived in Seoul to consult with ROK officials about Korean security following the January attacks. |
| April 18 | President Park held two rounds of talks with President Johnson in Honolulu. |
| May 28 | The first Korea-U.S. Defense Ministers meeting was held in Washington,D.C. |
| Dec. 23 | North Korea released the captain and crew of the Pueblo at Panmunjom after forcing an "apology" from the U.S. |

# 1969

| | |
|---|---|
| March 16 | Operation "Focus Retina" got underway in Yoju, Kyonggi Province in a combined ROK/US exercise. |
| July 31 | Secretary of State William P. Rogers arrived in Seoul for talks with Korean government leaders. |
| Aug. 20 | President Park left for the United States to hold talks with President Richard M. Nixon in San Francisco. |

# 1970

July 6      Secretary of State William Rogers proposed the initiation of consultations on U.S. troop reduction in Korea with the Seoul government.

Aug. 24     Vice President Spiro T. Agnew flew into Seoul for talks with President Park on U.S. troop reduction in Korea.

# 1971

March 4     The Korea-U.S. joint airborne and field exercise "Freedom Vault," a three-day war game south of Seoul, was launched.

March 27    The 7th U.S. Infantry Division left Korea following ceremonies at Eighth U.S. Army Headquarters in Seoul.

July 12     The first session of the two-day Korea-U.S. Security Consultative Meeting (SCM) was conducted in Seoul.

# 1972

March 1     Assistant Secretary of State Marshall Green arrived in Seoul to discuss President Richard M. Nixon's visit to Peking with President Park Chung Hee.

July 4      The seven-point joint communique was issued simultaneously in Seoul and Pyongyang.

Nov. 24     Korea and the U.S. signed a fishery cooperation agreement.

*U.S. President Gerald Ford and Korean President Park Chung Hee.*

# 1973

| | |
|---|---|
| March 28 | Korea and the U.S. initialed a double taxation avoidance agreement. |
| Sept. 7 | The U.N. Commission for the Unification and Rehabilitation for Korea (UNCURK) announced it had recommended in its annual report to the U.N. General Assembly that UNCURK be dissolved. |
| Nov. 16 | Secretary of State Henry Kissinger made a five-hour stopover in Korea for talks with President Park. |

# 1974

| | |
|---|---|
| Sept. 23 | The seventh session of the Korea-U.S. Security Consultative Meeting (SCM) was held in Honolulu. |
| Nov. 22 | President Gerald Ford arrived in Seoul for talks with President Park Chung Hee. |

# 1975

| | |
|---|---|
| Feb. 22 | U.N. Command, U.S. Forces Korea and Eighth U.S. Army were operationally combined under a single command. |
| June 26 | The Korea-U.S. Agreement concerning the trade of cotton fabrics, woolen textiles and man-made fiber products was signed. |
| Sept. 22 | U.S. Secretary of State Henry Kissinger proposed a conference of all parties directly involved in the Korean Armistice Agreement to the U.N. General Assembly. |

*North Korean soldiers attack unarmed American soldiers in the DMZ, killing two U.S. officers with axes.*

# 1976

| | |
|---|---|
| March 7-17 | The first "Team Spirit," a joint Korean-American military exercise, got underway in Korea. |
| July 22 | Secretary of State Henry Kissinger proposed a conference of South and North Korea, the United States and communist China to discuss the Korean question but received negative response from the communist side. |
| Aug. 18 | Two U.S. Army officers were brutally hacked to death in an unprovoked attack by some 30 axe-wielding North Koreans at Panmunjom. A work crew, supervised by the officers, were cutting a tree when attacked. |
| Sept. 6 | The U.S.-led U.N. Command and North Korea agreed on the division of the Joint Security Area of Panmunjom by the Military Demarcation Line (MDL). |
| Nov. 22 | A Korea-U.S. scientific and technological cooperation agreement was signed and went into force. |

# 1977

| | |
|---|---|
| March 9 | President Jimmy Carter announced that U.S. ground combat forces would be gradually pulled out of South Korea. |

March 19    President Carter called back Maj. Gen. John Singlaub, Chief of Staff, U.S. Forces Korea, who had voiced objection to Carter's plan to phase out U.S. troops in Korea. Singlaub was relieved of his Seoul post on May 21.

July 25     During his visit to Seoul, Secretary of Defense Harold Brown delivered a personal letter from President Jimmy Carter to President Park Chung Hee reaffirming America's defense commitment to South Korea.

Sept. 6     The U.S. Justice Department indicted Park Tong Sun, the key figure in the alleged "Korean influence-buying on Capitol Hill." The ROK-U.S. relations were already strained.

# 1978

May 24      Zbigniew Brzezinski, Assistant to President Carter for National Security Affairs, flew into Seoul to discuss Korea's national security efforts in connection with the proposed phase-out of U.S. ground forces.

Nov. 6      Secretary of Defense Brown arrived in Seoul for a three-day visit to discuss the security issue and to attend the activation ceremony of the Korea-U.S. Combined Forces Command (CFC). The CFC was formally activated on the following day.

Dec. 6      The U.S. House Ethics Committee closed its investigation of the so-called "Koreagate scandal."

Dec. 13     A group of 219 American soliders left for the U.S., the first U.S. ground combat troops to pull out of Korea.

# 1979

| | |
|---|---|
| June 1 | The "5,000 Years of Korean Art" exhibition was opened at San Francisco, beginning a two-year tour in the U.S. |
| June 29 | President Carter arrived in Seoul for a three-day state visit at the invitation of President Park. |
| July 20 | President Carter announced the suspension of the U.S. troop withdrawal. |

U.S. President Jimmy Carter during his visit to Korea.

| | |
|---|---|
| Oct. 26 | President Park was assassinated. A powerful American naval task force moved into the Korean strait to counter any possible North Korean plans to exploit the death of President Park. At the same time, the United States dispatched two AWACS aircraft to Korea. |
| Nov. 9 | The first Korea-U.S. Economic Policy Consultative Meeting was conducted in Seoul. |

# 1980

| | |
|---|---|
| March 11 | The Korea and U.S. defense authorities renamed I Corps (ROK/US) Group as the ROK-U.S. Combined Field Army. |

The 1980 Miss Universe Pageant in Seoul.

| | |
|---|---|
| July 8 | Miss U.S.A. Shawn Weatherly was crowned Miss Universe 1980 in the finale of the international beauty pageant held in Seoul. |
| Sept. 1 | Chun Doo Hwan was inaugurated as the Republic of Korea's new president. |
| Dec. 13 | President Chun and U.S. Secretary of Defense Brown discussed ways of strengthening Seoul-Washington cooperation. |

# 1981

| | |
|---|---|
| Jan. 28 | President Chun left for the United States at the invitation of President Ronald Reagan. |
| Feb. 2 | President Chun and President Reagan held summit talks at the White House. Chun was the first foreign head of state to meet with the new president. |
| April 28 | The 13th session of the Korea-U.S. Security Consultative Meeting (SCM) was held in San Francisco. |

Korean President Chun Doo Hwan and U.S. President Ronald Reagan meet in Washington.

| | |
|---|---|
| June 23 | A Korea-U.S. economic consultative meeting was conducted in Seoul to expand trade and economic cooperation between the two nations. |

# 1982

Jan. 17    The renovated Korean Friendship Bell Pavillion in Los Angeles County's Angels Gate Park was dedicated in a special ceremony and with a "certificate of property transfer" presented to Los Angeles Mayor Tom Bradley.

Jan. 25-27    The Korea-America Cultural Exchange Committee held its first meeting in Washington to discuss ways to facilitate cultural exchanges between the two nations.

March 28    U.S. Secretary of Defense Caspar W. Weinberger visited Korea and observed the Korean and American forces on the demilitarized zone and in the "Team Spirit '82" exercise. Weinberger also paid a courtesy call on President Chun Doo Hwan and attended the 14th Republic of Korea-United States Security Consultative Meeting.

April 26    Vice President George Bush visited Seoul and made a centennial commemoration speech before the Republic of of Korea National Assembly.

*U.S. Vice President George Bush at a centennial ceremony in Seoul.*

May 22    The centennial of ROK-U.S. diplomatic relations.

# Dedicated Efforts with Utmost Sincerity---
## That's the name of the game of Hyosung.

The Hyosung Group, noted for its dedication to perfection and for its loyalty to the customers, has thrived on textiles, tires, leather goods, lumbers, machinery, construction, heavy industries and general trading over the past three decades.

With an aim to become a more trust-worthy, business group with quality products and better services, Hyosung will strive to meet the needs of its clients the world over.

That's why we never cease to study, research, develop and improve ourselves to implant a true image of Hyosung within and without.

 HYOSUNG GROUP
**Represented by Hyosung Corporation**
C.P.O. BOX 1852 Seoul, Korea. CABLE: "HYOSTAR" SEOUL
TELEX: HYOSTAR K2312/5. TELEPHONE: 771-11

## OVERSEAS BRANCHES
•NEW YORK •LOS ANGELES •SEATTLE •HOUSTON •PANAMA •CARACAS •SANTIAGO •LONDON •STOCKHOLM •PARIS •FRANKFURT •LAGOS •CAIRO •JEDDAH •RIYADH •DAMMAM •AMMAN •TEHRAN •KUWAIT •COLOMBO •JAKARTA •SINGAPORE •HONG KONG •TAIPEI •SYDNEY •AUCKLAND •OSAKA •TOKYO

## MEMBERS OF THE HYOSUNG GROUP
•HYOSUNG CORPORATION •TONGYANG NYLON CO., LTD. •TONGYANG POLYESTER CO., LTD. •TOPLON CO., LTD. •TONGYANG DYEING CO., LTD.
•HYOSUNG HEAVY INDUSTRIES, LTD. •HYOSUNG ENGINEERING & CONSTRUCTION CO., LTD. •HYOSUNG SECURITIES CO., LTD. •TAESUNG LUMBER IND. CO.,LTD.
•WONMI APPAREL & TEXTILE LTD. •HANKOOK TIRE MFG. CO., LTD. •KOREA STORAGE BATTERY CO., LTD. •TAEJON LEATHER IND. CO., LTD.
•DONGSUNG CO., LTD. •DAESUNG CORPORATION •DONGSUNG CONSTRUCTION CO., LTD. •HYOSUNG DEVELOPMENT CO., LTD.
•KYUNGNAM DEVELOPMENT CO., LTD. •HYOSUNG MOTORS & MACHINERY, INC. •HYOSUNG ALUMINIUM CO., LTD. •HYOSUNG METAL PRODUCTS CO., LTD.
•HYOSUNG OIL CORPORATION •DONGSUNG DEVELOPMENT CO., LTD. •HYOSUNG-BASF CO., LTD. •HYOSAM CONTROL MAINTENANCE CO., LTD.
•HYOSUNG INSTRUMENT & ELECTRIC CO., LTD.

# Doosan has the products and the people to deliver satisfaction.

Doosan is becoming known far and wide for trade in a spirit of honesty and trust. These principles extend across the board through cooperation in product supplies both general and special, running the gamut from agricultural and fishery output to textiles, electronics, and military out-fitting. Whether your needs be these or others, the people at Doosan do everything to see that you are delivered with full satisfaction.

**ITEMS HANDLED**
BUILDING MATERIALS
ELECTRONICS
MILITARY EQUIPMENTS
FOODSTUFFS
GLASSWARE
LEATHER PRODUCTS
MACHINERY & HARDWARES
CAMPING GOODS
TEXTILE & GARMENTS
CHEMICALS
GENERAL MERCHANDISE

 **DOOSAN INDUSTRIAL CO., LTD.**
108-4, Susong-dong, Jongro-gu, Seoul Tel: 724-0016/9, 725-7121/6
Cable Add.: DOOSAN SEOUL Telex No. K23266, K23434

# TO BUILD A BETTER WORLD

Through honest endeavour and sheer hard work the people of Korea have made their country grow and prosper.

Now Korea is helping other people in other countries to build a better life for themselves.

The Dong Ah group is proud to be in the forefront of the many Korean companies who are active around the world.

In construction, shipping, trading, and engineering the Dong Ah flag flies high through-out the world.

Through professionalism, competitiveness and efficiency Dong Ah continues to pursue its ultimate aim.

To make the world a better place for people to live in.

# Learning from the past with eyes to the future.

**The Dolmen.**

One of the first structures erected by man. Its design, simple. Its materials, solid. Its workmanship, superb.

Today monuments like this are often looked back upon and admired by modern craftsmen and builders. Monuments that have withstood the ravages of time and served as a model from

which to build. A testimony to man's skill and ingenuity. A mark of quality.

Since 1946, we at Samwhan have been building the monuments of the future. Incorporating new methods and designs, advanced technology, economic efficiency and quality workmanship, we're building today for tomorrow's world.

## ⊕ SAMWHAN CORPORATION
## ⊕ SAMWHAN ENGINEERING

Chairman: Chong-Whan Choi

**HEAD OFFICE:** 98-20, Wooni-dong, Chongro-ku, Seoul, Korea. **C.P.O. Box** 42, Seoul. **Tel.:** 765-0151/9, 765-1871/9, 765-3741/9, 764-6111/9 **Cable:** GREENLIGHT SEOUL **Tlx.:** K28212, K24389, K25117 Overseas Branches: **MIDDLE EAST– Jeddah** Tlx.: 402411 SWCJED SJ **Riyadh** Tlx.: 201414 SAMWAN SJ **Dammam** Tel.: 83-27540 **Hodeidah** Tlx.: 5622 SWCHOD YE **Sana'a** Tlx.: 2383 SWCSNA YE **Amman** Tlx.: 21859 HOLINN JO
•**Asia–Jakarta** Tlx.: 46195 SAMNUCOIA **Singapore** Tlx.: SAMWHAN RS22086 **Manila** Tlx.: 27660 HLN PH **Tokyo** Tlx.: SAMWHAN J28363
•**U.S.A.–San Francisco** Tlx.: 278487 SWCUS UR. 171462 SWC SFO •**EUROPE–London** Tlx.: 8811588 SAMWHAN **Amsterdam** Tlx.: 10252 BPO NL

# The house of Ssangyong stands secure.

When we built Ssangyong we made sure that we stood on solid foundation.

Cement, oil refining, machinery, chemical manufacturing. . . .

These are the building blocks of a modern industrial society.

Through our dependability and the quality of our products, we have contributed to Korea's progress. But we haven't stopped there. Now you find us in more than a dozen enterprises. . . . marine shipping and transport, insurance construction, paper, engineering, electronics, and university, while sponsoring academic and cultural foundations. We export cement, fertilizers, iron and steel products, rolling stock, diesel engines, cars, motorcycles. . . . and much more. Customers from six continents have come to rely on us. Try us. You will agree.

**SSANG YONG SSANGYONG**

# Beautify your Home
# with furniture from HYUNDAI

All around the world, the quality of Hyundai Furniture is making a name for itself.

Hyundai Furniture is designed for strong and effective service, while making your living area a more comfortable and pleasant place at the same time.

From traditional to modern, Hyundai Furniture is certain to satisfy you with its own special style.

Hyundai experience, the most select timber and accessories, coupled with advanced coating technology and thorough quality control never fail to meet the exacting standards of even the most discriminating customer: in America, customer demand for quality furniture of early American style in K.D. has led Hyundai to establish its own assembly plant in Los Angeles.

You just can't find tougher, more dependable or more comfortable furniture than Hyundai. Why not let Hyundai help you make your home an even more beautiful and comfortable place to live?

 **HYUNDAI FURNITURE**

19401 SOUTH MAIN ST.
GARDENA CA. 90248
TEL.: 213-327—3394
TLX.: 910—346—7780
HDWOOD GDNA

# KOREA
## The Land of Living Treasure.

# Why are so many world travelers visiting Korea?

For those who have visited Korea, it is a place they long to return to. For those who have never experienced its delights, it offers exciting prospects. Korea well deserves to enjoy increasing popularity in the world of tourism. There are many images of Buddha whose sublime smile deeply touches the heart. Foreigners can never forget the heavenly smiles they meet for the first time. At the Folk Village, a living museum of Korean folklore, outside Seoul, tourists can get in touch with the traditional Korean way of living, including various kinds of traditional Korean dishes. Tourists can also visit the kilns where the world famous celadon porcelain of the Koryo Dynasty and white ceramics of Yi Dynasty are reproduced by the descendants of the ancient craftmen. Lovely scenery, fine accommodations, and charming gift items will add even more enjoyment to your tour of Korea.

Onward-bound orient clients can, for few hours of flight time beyond Tokyo or Hong Kong, with no additional air fare, stopover in Korea for up to 15 days without a visa. This is time enough for the basic Seoul-Kyongju-Cheju Island itinerary and to get a feel for the pulse of the country.

**KOREA NATIONAL TOURISM CORPORATION**
C.P.O. BOX 903 SEOUL, KOREA  TEL. 261-7001/6  TELEX: KOTOUR K28555

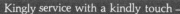

Kingly service with a kindly touch ——————

# From the Hotel with a Royal Tradition
## Best Wishes on the 100th Anniversary of Korean-American Relations
### Hotel Shilla, Seoul, Korea

In the 5,000 years of Korean history, the royal court of the Shilla Dynasty marked the height of national culture and refinement. Today, Hotel Shilla recaptures that elegant spirit by combining regal accomodations with service befitting a king.

Like attendants to royalty our multilingual staff is always there when you need them, adding a personal touch to hotel service that makes you feel as special as you really are. They are waiting to serve you in our seven international restaurants, 13 fully-equipped banquet and convention halls, and 672 spacious rooms and suites. They are at your call at our night club, poolside, and health club.

When you're in Seoul treat yourself to a brand of royal hospitality that you'll remember and return to again and again.

*Hotel Shilla*
Seoul, Korea
202, 2-Ga, Jangchung-Dong, Chung-Ku, Seoul, Korea
Tel: 255-3111, 3121, 3131, 3141, 4126
Cable: HOTEL SHILLA C.P.O. Box: 7000
Telex: SHILLA K24160, 24257

"1882-1982"
KOREA-U.S.A. TRADE CENTENNIAL

# Wherever you go, our best is always with you.

Everywhere Korean flies – to Southeast Asia, Japan, the Middle East, Africa, Europe and America – you'll go by B747 jumbo or other wide-bodied jet.

Whichever your destination, Korean will ease you there with traditional hospitality and courtesy.

Wherever you're bound, we'll be alongside with our best. So yours will be a flight in comfort, and so you'll pass the time with pleasure.

There are airlines and there are airlines. But why not treat yourself? To the one that sends all the best right along with you!

**We treat you as an honored guest.**

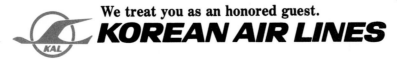

## KOREAN AIR LINES

# Your gateway to the Korean economy

South Gate, Korea's No. 1 National Treasure, was once the gateway to Korea. Today, KDB is also a gateway of sorts, a gateway to the Korean economy. With assets of over US$14 billion, we are Korea's largest bank and a national leader in the field of industrial financing. In fact, half of all capital investment loans to major Korean industries have been supplied by KDB. We also serve the Korean economy through a wide range of merchant banking activities. If you're looking to share in the dynamic Korean economy, KDB is your gateway to profit.

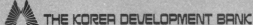 THE KOREA DEVELOPMENT BANK

I.P.O. Box 4570, Seoul, Korea Telex: K27463, K26544
Representative Office: Tokyo, London, New York, Hong Kong, Singapore, Frankfurt, Bahrain

Subsidiary: Korea Associated Securities Inc., New York
KDB International (Singapore) Ltd.

# BRINGING KOREA TO YOUR DOORSTEP

With 38 overseas offices located in the leading business centers of the world, Korea Exchange Bank provides a truly global service.

We not only serve our country's economic development but also offer overseas customers a unique insight into the Korean market.

We are ideally placed to identify the areas of maximum profit opportunity for your company and to assist in overcoming the practical difficulties of developing an unfamiliar market and provide high quality financial services specially tailored to meet your requirements.

## KOREA ✦ EXCHANGE BANK
### — KOREA'S LEADING BANK —

**Head Office:** C.P.O. Box 2924 Seoul, TELEX NO. K24244, K24245, K27237, K27254, Cable Address: KOEXBANK SEOUL Tel: 771-46

# GOLD STAR
# STRIPE

## A 20-year histo

We at Gold Star have come a long way since we established Korea's electronics industry back in 1958. And we believe that we owe a great part of this progress to the American people.

When we first started exporting to the United States in the early 60s, we never dreamed that you would receive Gold Star products so enthusiastically. Because of your response, we established a separate affiliate company, Gold Star Electronics International, Inc., to handle sales and service to the growing Gold Star family. As the family began to grow even larger, we set up regional offices in Chicago and Los Angeles to be sure that both Gold

THE QUALITY CHOICE
## GOLD STAR

**GOLD STAR CO., LTD.**   C.P.O. BOX 2530 SEOUL, KOREA.
TEL.: 753-3970, TELEX; GSRADIO K23751/5 SEOUL

# AND FOREVER!

## that deserves a Gold Star.

Star dealers and customers received the best possible service. All this in response to your obvious faith in our products.

Last year we established our most recent endeavor in the United States, Gold Star of America, a manufacturing facility located in Huntsville, Alabama. The GSAI plant will produce color televisions with American skilled labor and Korean technology, a monument to the 100 years of friendship that our two countries have shared.

At Gold Star we're very proud of the progress we've made and the 20 years of our history that we've been able to share with you, the American people.

As festivities and ceremonies take place across the United States and Korea, we hope that you'll remember that we, the people of Korea think that each and every one of you deserve a gold star for friendship.

# SMIB

**SMIB, both as a development finance institution and a commercial bank, specializes in assisting small and medium industries in Korea to play a bigger role in the growth of Korea economy.**

**Major Services**

- General Banking Services
- International Banking Services
- Foreign Currency Loan Relendings
- Equity Investment Operations
- Credit Information Operations
- Extension Services

 **The Small and Medium Industry Bank**

Head Office: 36-1, 2-ka, Ulchi-ro, Choong-ku, Seoul, Korea
Telephone: 771-50, 776-6811, 776-6821
Cable Address: "MEDINDBANK" Seoul
New York Representative Office: 375 Park Avenue, Suite 2608
New York, N.Y. 10152 U.S.A.
Telex: 237144 SMIBK, UR Telephone: 212-980-3353
Tokyo Representative Office: Room 524, Yurakucho Bldg. 10-1
Yurakucho 1-Chome Chiyoda-ku Tokyo 100, Japan
Telex: 02228350 SMIBKJ Telephone: 03-287-0335~6

# THE CBK IS PROGRESSING AHEAD

Based on a policy of sincerity and diligence which has
been on display for 83years, we are constantly progressing
ahead in every banking aspect by introducing innovative
ways to do business and by uniting the korean will with
those of the other nations of the world.

The CBK, making progress in the world stage with its solid
position at home, would like to be your good neighbor.

**THE COMMERCIAL
BANK OF KOREA**

P.O.Box Central 126, Seoul, Korea
Telex : K24611-6
Tel –771-30

# For your business with KOREA
# ask KOREA FIRST BANK first.

KOREA FIRST is already a half-century tradition, offering complete domestic banking services in over 115 branches in cities and towns throughout Korea. Now KOREA FIRST is serving customers in countries all over the world as well, through its network of nine overseas branches and more than 1,000 correspondent banks.
So if you're looking for a bank with the most reputable of connections in Korea, and known for efficiency, come to KOREA FIRST.
KOREA FIRST-where 'first' means the best in speedy, unerring, and kind service to you.

Head Office : 53-1, 1-ga, Chungmu-ro, Jung-gu, Seoul 100 Korea       Cable Address : FIRST BANK SEOUL
TLX : K23758, K24249, K24479, K26535, K23685, K23759, K25363, K25364,       TEL : 776-6141

Chicago Br.: TLX : 206090 Chicago TEL : 312-663-3560   /   London Br.: TLX : 889350 London TEL : 01-626-9264   /   L.A. Agency :
TLX : 688454 Los Angeles TEL : 213-625-7700   /   N.Y. Agency : TLX : RCA 238144, WUI 668115, WUD 640137 New York   TEL :
212-593-2525   /   Osaka Br. : TLX : J63892 Osaka TEL : 06-649-4941   /   Tokyo Rep.: TLX : J23329 Tokyo TEL : 03-201-6261   /
Hong Kong Rep. :  Korea First Finance Ltd.  (Hong Kong) : TLX : 85962 Hong Kong TEL : 5-265025   /
Singapore Rep.: TLX : RS20853 TEL : 224-8477

**KOREA FIRST BANK**

Tulip is a symbolic flower of SEOULTRUST

# Where to go to do business in Korea .

It's definitely SEOULTRUST which is the largest commercial bank in Korea with over US$ 11 billion in total assets and the only bank authorized to handle trust business in Korea, dealing with deposits, loans and foreign exchange business as well.

But our size means the least proud one to us and doesn't make us impersonal.

Holding 146 branches in Korea, increasing overseas network and international correspondents covering major parts of the world, SEOULTRUST can put its full range of domestic and international banking capabilities to work for you whenever you need them.

Have a talk with SEOULTRUST and take a step ahead in your business with Korea.

# ⊗ BANK OF SEOUL AND TRUST COMPANY

**HEAD OFFICE:** 10-1,NAmdaemun-ro,2-ka,Chung-ku,Seoul 100,Korea.Mail Box:C.P.O.Box 276 Tel.:771-60 Telex:K23311/5 Cable:SEOULTRUST
**OVERSEAS NETWORK:** NEW YORK, LOS ANGELES, HOUSTON, LONDON, FRANKFURT/MAIN, HONG KONG,TOKYO, SINGAPORE.

# FIND KOREA JUST BESIDE YOU

The 1982 World's Fair!
Visiting the Korea Pavilion at the Knoxville International
Energy Exposition will be a great experience for you.
KOTRA, organizing the Korea Pavilion cordially invites you
to the "New Horizon in Korea."

# 韓國外國語大學校

## HANKUK UNIVERSITY OF FOREIGN STUDIES

270-1 Rimoon-Dong, Dongdaemoon-Ku, Seoul, 131, Korea (Tel.) 967-1811/20

*Chairman Board of Trustee.*
*Dr. Kim, Heung Bae*

*President*
*Dr. Kim, Dong Son*

## *Establishment of Yongin Campus*

This is the first step of the expansion program of the Univeristy. In the future, the campus will be expanded to 800,000 pyeong with a building area 150,000 pyeong. The University will eventually have ten colleges and five graduate schools with an enrollment capacity of 36,000 students.

# A winning combination:
## Experienced people & high technology

The Samsung basketball team is the best in Korea. We organized the best talents available and drilled them into a team that is unbeatable. We used the same formula to build the 95,000 member Samsung work force that now enjoys a worldwide reputation for advanced technological know-how and reliability.

In ventures that have taken us into everything from general foodstuffs to sophisticated industrial plants, the people in the 26 Samsung companies have proven themseleves able to compete with high technology leaders throughout the world. The Samsung companies now specialize in a wide range of business lines that includes foreign trade, heavy and chemical industries, electronics, precision instruments, construction, petrochemicals, and others.

When you deal with Samsung you truly deal with a team – a team that is able to face tasks together if the job calls for it, and a team that can save you time, money, and worry.

We're proud of all 95,000 members of the Samsung team and they're proud of themseleves. They know they are among the best and they are getting better.

## SAMSUNG GROUP

**Represented by Samsung Co., Ltd.**
C.P.O. Box 1144 Seoul, Korea
Telex:STARS K23657/K23302/K23349
Cable Address: STARS SEOUL

**OVERSEAS BRANCHES:**

| | | | | | |
|---|---|---|---|---|---|
| TOKYO | Tel: (03) 581-7511/7, Tlx: SAMSTARS J24244 | NEW YORK | Tel: (201) 592-7900, Tlx: 135536 SAMSUNG FORT | MILANO | Tel: (02) 800106, Tlx: 313390 MILSTA I |
| OSAKA | Tel: (06) 266-0752/5, Tlx: STARSK J64322 | LOS ANGELES | Tel: (213) 936-8111, Tlx: 696141 LASTAR LSA | LAGOS | Tel: 611060, Tlx: 21808 STARS NG |
| HONG KONG | Tel: H-234369, Tlx: 83236 HSTAR HX | HOUSTON | Tel: (713) 960-1910, Tlx: 79-0107 SAMSUNG HOU | KUWAIT | Tel: 416632, Tlx: SAMSTARS 2764 KT |
| KUALA LUMPUR | Tel: 488510, Tlx: MA 30856 KULSTA | PANAMA | Tel: 69-3533, Tlx: 2467 PANASTAR PG | TEHRAN | Tel: 622141, Tlx: 215145 SMC IR |
| SINGAPORE | Tel: 433143, Tlx: STARSIN RS 23700 | BUENOS AIRES | Tel: 392-2305, Tlx: 18840 STARS AR | RIYADH | Tel:4643587, Tlx: 200543 ANCOD SJ |
| SYDNEY | Tel: (02) 241-2241, Tlx: STARSY AA 26428 | CARACAS | Tel: 33-4681, Tlx: 21201 VEGRA | JEDDAH | Tel: 6431544, Tlx: 402537 JAMSTA SJ |
| RANGOON | Tel: 71417, Tlx: 21201 TELBOX BM | MEXICO | Tel: 516-71-20, Tlx: 1772647 BEIME (MEXICO) | DAMMAM | Tel: 8330447, Tlx: 601456 GESCO SJ |
| JAKARTA | Tel: 324759, Tlx: 45120 SAMSUNG IA | SANTIAGO | Tel: 397718, Tlx: 94635 SAMSTA, KU | CAIRO | Tel: 910880, Tlx: 92817 HOILD UN |
| BANGKOK | Tel: 233-5007, Tlx: 87961 STARBKK TH | LONDON | Tel: (01) 831-6951, Tlx: 264606 STARS LG | DUBAI | Tel: 229634, Tlx: 46828 ALSAM EM |
| MANILA | Tel: 817-63-12, Tlx: 22648 STARS PH | FRANKFURT | Tel: (0611) 740841, Tlx: 0416479 SMCF D | TRIPOLI | Tel: 39186, Tlx: 20543 STACON LY |
| DACCA | Tel: 238619, Tlx: 65614 STAR BJ | PARIS | Tel: 538-6836, Tlx: STAR PAR 250730 F | BAHRAIN | Tel: 233499, Tlx: 8291 BASAM BN |
| NEW DELHI | Tel: NEW DELHI 42905, Tlx: 031-3825 MOST IN | DÜSSELDORF | Tel: (0211) 320014, Tlx: 8686392 SAMD D | AMMAN | Tel: 42182, Tlx: 21867 METE JO |